In the Crucible of My Catharsis

By Thomas Fullmer

(Cover photo from Pixabay.com)
(Edited by Rose Terranova Cirigliano)
Published by

QUEENS BROOKLYN LONDON
ROME SAN FRANCISCO

DEDICATION

To Barbara, we all miss you so much!

EDITOR'S INTRODUCTION

by Rose Terranova Cirigliano

"God, grant me the serenity to accept the things I can not change..."
- St. Francis of Assisi

In Thomas Fullmer's newest collection of poems, In the Crucible of My Catharsis, we are immersed with Thomas in his internal world as he moves through the difficult process of accepting that which he can not change; the loss of his wife, and all the regrets and guilt that he feels.

This is not a book to be read quickly.

Rather, it needs to be read and re-read, and contemplated. Write in the margins, if need be. Savor the breath of his words as they gush across the page in a torrent of passion and emotion, filled with longing and yearning, as he searches the depths of his soul for answers and healing and release from the chains of the anguish he is overwhelmed by from the loss of his love, his wife.

Hear his testimony of the inner battle and soul searching process flooding the pages. Pause often, and reflect. Share it with a friend.

In His Own Words
from the author

Thomas Fullmer is the author of several books, including his book of poetry, From the Fabric of My Mind. This is his second book of poetry. In his first book of poetry he spoke of his love for his wife, and the loss he felt after her passing away in September 2019. This book of poetry continues on that vein in celebrating her life and the love they shared. They reflect his own suffering through the lonely hours of his life after losing her. The title In the Crucible of My Catharsis is a poignant reminder of how we all deal with loss. It is truly a test of faith, in trying to cope with life after all hope seems gone. Truly the passing of treasured loved ones brings such pain, sometimes more than we feel we can bear. Many of the poems in this book were written after Fullmer's wife's death, and so truly reflect his attempt to put the pieces of a shattered life together, and carry on without his beloved wife. The poems are truly a type of catharsis, for in writing many of these poems he dealt with his own pain, and found relief. Emotionally charged and highly spiritual in nature, Fullmer hopes his poetry will touch the hearts and lives of readers everywhere. He wants his poetry to be a source of healing for those who have experienced tragic loss in their lives. Writing the poems helped Fullmer emote and deal with his loss, he hopes it helps others deal with theirs. Suffering seems to be a common theme in Fullmer's writings. From the time when he grew up as a little boy in central Utah, to the recent loss of his wife, Fullmer's life has always been full of tribulation. As Fullmer says, "Sometimes I write a poem, and then I go back and read it, it brings tears to my eyes. I wonder how something so poignant came out of such a broken down old man as me. I think, maybe it's because I bleed my pain onto the page." For it is in the crucible of our own catharsis that we truly grow, and thereby find redemption. .

TABLE OF CONTENTS

The Substance of Things Past

The Substance

Definition of substance.
1a : essential nature : essence.
b : a fundamental or characteristic part or quality.
2a : ultimate reality that underlies all outward manifestations and change.

Invisible

Do you see me?
I am substance
none wish to see
pain created me
my non-existent state
is a convenient lie
meant to erase me
wandering as it were
trapped in my crucible
called time
space does not exist
within this separation
shorn of physical manifestations
what is there to manifest?
I am as invisible to you
as the tau neutrino
interacting with nothingness
it is too convenient
to sweep me aside
to devalue my
supposed existence
to treat me as dross
even dross has substance
you rob me of my reality
you obliterate my identity
you refuse to recognize me
to you I am invisible
conveniently invisible
can invisible hands compose truth?
words do not appear out of nowhere
not even the uncertainty principle
can define that probability
I write truth so you might see

my essence is corporeal
your reality is mirrored in me
invisible to your dismissive eyes
I function amidst shadows
cast by your vindictive nature
into the nether regions of obscurity
I slink behind a drawn veil
part this tattered curtain
to reveal the crucible
of your own existence
mirrored in me
when you erase me
you erase yourself
refusal to acknowledge
we are bound together by reality
leads to self-annihilation
salvation rests in your realization
we are bound by perfect love

Truth to Heal

there are truths to be learned from our lives
truths that heal wounds from vicious lies
lies caused by those who choose
to mythologize evil
good cannot come when we ignore
true experience
or choose belief in lies
from evil's we know exist
the morning sun rises to evaporate
dew on blades of grass
the alley cat prowls after the mouse or rat
only to eat refuse instead
the mule deer doe feeds
in mountain meadow with fawn nearby
the rainbow trout leaps forth
from the mountain pond to nab gnats
the mountains fill with winter snow
melt feeds brooks, rivers, and lakes
farms receive water diverted
by irrigation canals, ditches, and furrows
the sparrow hawk circles overhead
in search of sparrows on which to descend
hay, grain, and corn grow
towards the bounty of harvest time
cows, pigs, and sheep await
truckloads of gifts from farmers' fields
food is laid upon the table for consumption
refuse feeds the alley cat
the cycle of life turns, connected in a web
nothing is a universe unto itself
to accept this is to know the reality
of an existence where entropy rules
no good was ever served by believing in lies,

no soul was thereby healed

falsehoods within a family are inbred
from realities too harsh to acknowledge
a monster, in the guise of a man
terrorizes his wife and children
some may never experience
the reality of the savagery
others come to know
over time, these desire to ignore
that such family secrets exist
lies are spread to create mythology
never reflective of true savagery
the monster who ruled with iron fist
is canonized a saint instead
what serves truth?
the mythologized saint created
for familial pain avoidance?
or the realization and acceptance
a monster ruled with fear, instead?
not even the brutal monster is served
by his misdeeds covered in lies
it is like covering a pearl of great price
in a pile of manure
no healing can ever come
by twisting reality into false dreams
the dream has always been a nightmare
for those who endured
I do not wake up in the middle of the night
with screams when fists descend
because the abuse I endure was merely myth
my childhood monsters were real
it does not remove pain
to pretend that what I endured
and witnessed was unreal

opinion cannot redefine truth
it cannot change the reality
of my experience
because it lacked its own experience

the cruel brute remains to haunt
the shadows of my mind with savagery
my brokenness can never be healed
except by the balm of truth
truth is a tonic for the tortured soul
a fountain of healing waters
no vessel can ever be healed
to be filled with perfect love if lies rule
only truth can heal a broken vessel
broken by a monster's atrocity
only a whole vessel can be filled
with pure and perfect love, even charity
only pure and perfect love
can heal tormented souls broken by lies
great evil is done by allowing
lies to mythologize a brute into a saint
truth is the only power to heal
truth will cleanse and heal a broken soul
truth heals the ties that bind
connections within families
between mankind
truth will lead to sweet fountains
of pure and perfect love
the only source of true joy
is acceptance of love born of truth
let all the lies be damned to Hell!
Accept truth, or be damned as well!
I will never accept another's attempt
to mythologize the source of my deepest pain
which I know exists inside

I accept truth of all I know
just as I accept the cold of winter snow
I accept truth as through the forest thicket
I gaze upon a doe and fawn
I accept truth as I circle the cool waters
of a trout filled pond
I accept truth as I look through mists of rain
to mountains beyond
I accept truth as I gaze across farms
full of amber waves of grain
through the window of my car
even when I am lost in my pain
I accept truth as I can see the shadow
of the sparrow hawk circle in the sky
I accept truth when I realize
the brutality of my youth is no myth
it's not a lie
there are those I love
who would change the nature of reality
they sweep truth under the rug of life
and from it flee
it does not change brutality's source
of my childhood reality
only acceptance of truth will change
the course of what my life will be
I accept truth as my guide
to interpret reality now, and for all eternity

True Love Endures

like icy glaciers feed
streams and rivers
to fill lakes and ponds
eventually oceans below
cause green things to grow
so does true love endure
the ravages of time
to feed the parched gardens
of our tortured souls
true love brings
evolutionary transformation

passion burns as a hot ember
boiling up into a paroxysm
of volcanic eruption
fervent heat consumes lovers
fuses bodies, entwined in rapture

evolutionary transformation
brings true love from
the brink of annihilation
to the warmth of compassion
like wrapping up in a warm blanket
when the cold hand of winter
hits like a wall of ice
in one arctic blast
chilled to the bone
compassion warms the soul

the warmth of compassion
brings the eternal spring
in the midst of frozen winter
hope is lost, like a ship

caught in the grip
of Antarctic ice
desolation all around
true love springs forth
to melt the frozen heart
more beautiful than before
to sing the heart song
as the lark bursts forth
in joyous rapture
like the blue tailed butterfly
bursting forth from its cocoon

true love descends beneath
the deepest, darkest realm
of the lowest hell
wanders through
the parched desolation
of the waterless desert
crosses the widest ocean
baked beneath the hottest sun
salt water all around
no wind, no hope
never a drop to drink
until true love
brings sweet rain of compassion in a deluge

true love endures all
in its transformation
brokenness is healed
a strong vessel formed
cleanse the inner vessel
preparatory to evolving Into...

brokenness healed
shattered heart healed

cracked mind healed
torn soul healed
a pure vessel formed
like fusing pottery shards
together to form
a perfect vase of antiquity
this vessel, when cleansed
through purification's process
filled with perfect love
the very power of creation
evolutionary transformation
proconsul evolves into dreamers
to experience pure love's healing power
as pure love evolves into
the embodiment of perfect love
the only power capable of moving
heaven and earth
and save the soul of man
pure love is perfect love in embryo

perfect love endures into the eternities
for all things must fail
except pure and perfect love
it is the love of Christ upon the cross
the love of Buddha under the Lotus tree
the love of Mohammed to recite
the love of Nephi to guide through a desert
love guides the way of truth and right
light through the deepest, darkest night
greatest of all the gifts of God
greatest power in the universe
power by which universes
and all they are come into being
the word was spoken
the word was "love"

passion can burn up
in a blink of an eon's eye
poof! Gone!
only love endures
speak not of the glory of love
unless your love
has endured
the ravages of time

as the acorn
grows into the mighty oak
so pure love evolves
into perfect love
nothing else endures
nothing else heals
nothing else creates
nothing else matters
salvation is perfect love
eternal life is perfect love
love evolves
perfect love its final step
in the evolutionary chain of love

look within to find love's spark
see as God sees
know as God knows
love as God loves

eternal truth of love and light
exist within the soul
it is here you must go
to learn, to know
to find the well spring
of pure and perfect love
let healing waters flow

Casualties of Life

these casualties of life
these walking wrecks of human flesh
derailed from life's purpose
by the pitfalls of society's vicious hand
ambushed by desire run amuck
left to wander the streets
as soulless victims
of a world gone insane
for pleasures of the moment
indulgence of the flesh
and appetites for perversion
for that which cannot satisfy
but leaves them in a dark void
a wasteland of souls
where evil cries:
hear them gnash!
hear them wail!
wail and gnash
gnash and wail!
restless souls alive in Hell

If They Fall

pestilence of old
consumes society
leaves men spirit blind
too blind to discern truth from error
too hobbled to walk in straight and true paths
unaware they step dangerously close to an abyss
if they fall, they will never return
build upon a true foundation
with faith in He who is mighty to save
they will never fall
but drink of a well spring of water
springing forth unto eternal life

Lost in Barren Wasteland

you are the Sahara
where I can find no drink
for there is nothing there
but barren sand
and dry suffocating heat
under the torment
of a conflagration of fused power
that leaves you dry
leaves me parched and dying
hopelessly void of anything to quench
my ravenous thirst from bone dry throat
I wander in you lost in torment
forlorn in a wilderness of dearth and death
hopeless in a barren wasteland
surrounded by hot, dry earth
scorched sun overhead
not a drop of cool refreshing liquid in sight
nothing to quench my aching thirst
to keep my heart and soul alive
I shrivel up and die

Battle Cry of Perversion

battle cry of immoral freedom
rings throughout the land
like the wailing of damned souls
gnashing teeth exclaim:
"Whatever perversion for our diversion
we claim our right to choose
even if the sanctity of heart and soul we lose."

trouble brews upon the land
noxious concoction made of man
philosophy poisons society as a whole
untouched, unsullied, or unmarred
by this pitiless cry for freedom for perversion
let freedom ring throughout the land
bells toll for the passing pyre
of the spiritually dead:
"Now is the age of unfettered perversion
upon the face of the land!"
Is it a victory cry or the pitiful wail?
moribund society gone to Hell

thrust off perversion's chains
or the few will bind the whole
Hear the spiritually blind
gnash and wail:
"It is our inalienable right to destroy self!
To reinterpret reality in any way we choose!
To create truth out of lies!"
If so, do you have the right to destroy us too?
Will the moral many become the virtuous few?

What is Love?

Is love the twitching between a young man's legs
as he gazes longingly at a porno magazine
Is love the desire in a husband's heart
for the woman lying next to him in bed, his wife
when he doesn't even care anything about her
except how he can ravage her body this night
Is love the make up sex of a couple
who have torn each other verbally to shreds
ending with an exchange of hard slaps
before they fall into each other's arms
as they reach for ecstasy
is love the taking or the giving
an emotion or an action
the soft beating of the heart when two are apart

What is Love?
can we make rhyme or reason out of this enigma
and call it what we will when we choose to say that
"I am in love with you?"
or is it suffering and anguish
as you sit by the sick bed of a dear one in need
and offer a little prayer for the suffering to cease
can Webster define love in adequate terms
are all encompassing, reflective of the emotion
poets write about love while feeling all the time
we are inadequate to the task.
is love a hallmark card with someone else's
interpretation heart's desire written inside
is it making love in bed
achieving orgasmic climax
and then holding each other close
even though love's vows have never been spoken
or is it the fireman who dashes into a burning building

to save just one more child as the building falls down
trapping both inside to courageously die
Or is it a God hung upon a tree,
for witnesses to record His love eternally

I ask: what is love?
is it what we think it is, or is it so much more
if we could find an answer to this question
maybe then we would end the suffering
in the world, the depravation, and the death
when one is all alone and has nothing but
sickness to keep her company
find an answer to love's quandary
and you will have solved the great mystery of life
We are creatures of love
it is a very human thing
But what in the end does all that really mean?

Walk in My Love

walk in the light of my sweet love
feel warmth in every heartbeat
angelic light cascades down from above
descends through despair, souls greet
gentle touch on your lovely face
my voice lifts you from dark abyss
kiss of wind, dark shadows erase
bodies close to sense lover's bliss
you are a cool Summer's breeze
cool my brow, my body tease
your body close, sensations please
we sit on summer swing in ease
autumn seems but a breath away
your voice upon my heartstrings plays
lingers near is scent of new mown hay
in each other's arms, no longer strays
we watch the setting of sun, blood red
I gaze deep into your velvet eyes
moths cackle in bug zapper overhead
slowly, I begin to stroke your thighs

War

we wage a war against evil, wherever it is found
wars for our very souls, wars against the ills of society
poverty is rampant in all its forms
from the cardboard shack of a homeless mother
into the spiritual malaise we all too often wander
where to go? Which way to turn?
corruption in governments consumes hope, feeds greed
predators stand on every corner our lives wander around
waiting to descend upon us like hyenas descending upon fresh meat

perversion distorts reality, like gazing through opaque mirrors
mirrors of eternity shattered, their credibility betrayed
perversion flows from Satan's vile tongue
always false, always evil
Hitler spoke of ubermench
when his only true goal was to destroy mankind
drag society through the gutter of Nazi swill
too many would be leaders do little better
spewing forth their poison like a gusher of toxic waste
extremism lead to poles so disparate, society will break in two
where is balance? Where is sanity?

break chains of evil, discard vile thoughts
reject falsehoods wherever they exist
pull them out by their noxious roots
embrace God's truth instead
such is our only hope
only by this can society be healed
to be one with the divine, one with God
one with his purpose

which God?
what purpose?

find your fountain of truth to drink
only then is your mind open to this truth
God has left a piece of himself in you
we are his spiritual creations
when you touch the life of others
you leave a piece of yourself in their souls
there are pieces of others within you
they can be your guiding lights
be wary they are not false lights
the pathway of truth leads to eternal life
it is the pathway to God

a pathway paved with faith, hope, charity, and love
follow it with singleness of heart

be guided to find self-truth, to realize self-fulfillment
it is the pathway to our fountains of eternal truths
whose waters we must imbibe
where we can embrace hope, achieve peace
look within to discover your own fountain of truth
it might lie beneath your life's rubble
dig deep to uncover it, there are no free rides
drink deep and live, or let your soul thirst and die
look within to discover your inner truth
open your heart and let your fountain of truth flow free

Connected

as the Andean condor
floats past glaciated peaks
we are connected

as the timber wolf's howl
Is married to the harvest moon
we are connected

as the golden eagle of the rocky Gobi
swoops down upon a bounding Jerboa
we are connected

as the heat of day melts into the velvet night
the barn owl spies the scurrying meadow vole
we are connected

as the winter melt
brings the robin's song
we are connected

as the blue tailed butterfly's proboscis
dips deep into golden marigolds
we are connected

as the pounding waves upon the rocky shore
causes the cackling gulls to argue incessantly
we are connected

as a robin feeds her squawking hatchlings
clamor to eat worms from her own beaked mouth
we are connected

as the red tail hawk swoops low
snatches a fleeing grey squirrel
we are connected

as the beaver fells trees with gnawing teeth
creates a pond filled with glacier melt
we are connected

as lake trout break the mirrored surface
feast upon dragonflies and mosquitoes
we are connected

as the winter snows feed roaring rivers
quench parched lands for grain to thrive
we are connected

as a meadowlark rest upon a fence
warbles its greeting to the breaking dawn
we are connected

as the autumn chill brings brilliant strewn leaves
cover frosted ground in reds, yellows, oranges, and
fuchsias
we are connected

as fusion of elements within a fireball in the sky
brings warmth to a blue-green planet
we are connected

as a mother kneels to comfort her crying toddler
a hand reaches out to sprinkle survival at her feet
we are connected

as pointe shoes leap and pirouette
transform black swan into white
we are connected

as a mother holds her tiny infant in gentle arms
the memory of labor pain lost in this beatific moment
we are connected

as an electron leaps from its orbital position
resultant Eigenvalues determine reality, cause change
we are connected

as the universe's laws spin towards two-point-seven
Kelvin
the resultant "Big Chill" maximum entropy
we are connected

as one hand is exhilarated by another
two melt into one with a stroll into a poetic sunset
we are connected

as a cherished loved one lies eaten by cancer
a tender hand brings a sip of water to trembling lips
we are connected

connections cross boundaries
connections pass on cultural traditions
connections share cultural truths
connections bring us close
connections define us as human
we are connected by perfect love
so why don't we love perfectly?

we are connected
we do not fully understand
certain inner truths
connections to the spiritual
which engenders deep emotions
manifested in space-time as words upon this page
my flimsy attempt to express truth
these truths I treasure
Will you treasure them too?
so you and I might be connected

When I Said

When I said that I loved you, what did I really mean?
not to cause you pain my dear, the suggestion is obscene
I wanted to be with you, hold you in my arms
kiss your tender lips, protect you from all harm

emotional distance is so vast, it's full of so many doubts
all we had was distance shared over which we could not shout
you lived in your sweet world, I existed in mine
it didn't seem we'd come together, our lives to intertwine

distance was too great, the loneliness even more
I had to leave my love, I had to shut the door
it wounded you, it wounded me, a chasm it created
I had to for survival's sake, a reason that I hated

you ask me to open the door and let your love back in
your love is still in my heart, though that might be a sin
you see I want too much, much more than you will ever give
my love we'll stay apart and try to go on and live

the best we can with broken hearts separate are we two
know forever in my heart, my darling I love you
we shared so much not long ago, but let it now be
maybe we'll have another chance in eternity

I will never hold you gentle hand
darling can't you please understand
this pain that torments me inside
pain of longing for you that I did hide

our time has come and gone
no prize between us was ever won
let us go our separate way
start a brand new day

Your Memory

your memory is an artesian well from which I long to drink
your memory is a sinkhole in which I desire to sink
to wrap myself in your mind's blanket, keep me warm inside
to draw your body next to mine, and from you never hide
I dreamt of you, so very close, held deep within my grasp
your love's intoxicating venom from fangs sunk like an asp
feel your bite deep into my flesh, cause my passion to whine
to feel your body's memory fit perfectly with mine
to walk treasured paths with you, to know your love once more
to feel your hunger stir within, I enter your mind's door
let flames of fire ignite your body in a rapturous fire
this memory of your passion deep I'll sip, of you I'll never tire

Your Feminine

I arouse your body's curiosity
my hardened heat chases within your womb
our separate parts hot with the flame of life
united we burst together
we cascade forth into microscopic
bursts of flame, fuse our two into one
fused by fire, knit by flame
entwined bodies join our souls
like fervent serpents who copulate to create
hearts beat in rhythm as one
like a perfectly composed piano sonata
my harmony intertwined with your melody just so
we taste, drink, and smell our shared deliciousness
we sate our thirst by imbibing love nectar as it flows
this fire of life as divine beings breath
makes desperate whole and complete
we are a marriage of flames
my masculine, your feminine
we are fused by heat
within your feminine
from which life springs
beatific life unique and complete
we find volcanic release

your feminine heat
your feminine fire
your feminine energy
culmination of all my desires is
YOU...
my masculine within your feminine
to find salvation in your arms

If…

If you gaze deep within my soul
see things I don't want you to know
would you see my secrets I hide deep within?
my darkest moments I try to hide, my sins
there is inner truth we both long to discover
yours in you, and mine in me

would you see the time I broke Mom's clock
blamed it on baby brother?
babies break things, Right!
Mom just didn't seem to care
would she have cared if she knew it was me

what about the many times I took quarters
to buy comic books, Disney and Dennis the Menace?
the bag I'd gathered quarters in was so full
soon it was too empty, others knew
but few consequences were ever paid except within my
soul

there are so many fears in me
look! You might see, these dark fears
the time I would not let go of the roof of the old house
I clung for dear life, though the ground was inches away
yellow bricks covered the ground, I was afraid to trip
I was afraid I'd fall back and break my crown
Mom had to help me down, my brothers laughed

I could never be a bird, I would find it so absurd
though I love to see Andean Condors fly past snowy
peaks

I liked to climb trees, there was a treehouse fashioned of
scrap wood
I would climb elm trees, pluck the leaves, chew them,
headache gone
rooftops terrified me, I could never fly, I was not meant
to be a bird

look inside of me to see the monsters that haunted my
dreams
I tried to climb out of the basement window and flee
my feet would not carry me, they felt like bars of steel
I felt like my feet were sinking into the ground, into
quicksand

the old oil furnace came alive in deep winter with a rattle
and a groan
next to my bedroom, it was a terrifying monster of my
imagination
when it awoke on a cold January night, so did I, in terror

If fears were all you could see when you gazed inside of
me
it would be no big deal, there are worse things than
childhood fears
maybe you'd see the spirit of hope Dad tried to kill
he didn't
he couldn't
I wouldn't let him
not completely, just a little, but too much, always too
much

I hoped
I dreamed
maybe you could see the remnants of those hopes and
dreams

like finding shattered and scattered shards of pottery
from bygone civilizations conquered by another
sift and glue the shards together to recreate a lovely vase
or a decorated plate of Nabatean fine red wares unveiled

I had lovely hopes
I had lovely dreams
look inside to find the shards strewn across my life
if you put them together, you might find the beauty in me
the goodness, the beautiful vulnerability you came to see
maybe that's the real me
maybe it's all me
just look, if you want to see

if you find something loathsome and abhorrent
do not be afraid, like the rabbit racing before the fox
do not be filled with dismay
like a swimmer in an ocean pulled down by
undercurrents
we all have monsters and demons lurking inside
we all have our crosses to bear
byproducts of oppression
you will find sweet memories, as well
like drinking from a sweet artesian well
stuff of joy and laughter to make your heart swell

we are all a mosaic of experiences
some dark and dreary
like a cold waste land at twilight
void of life, love, and hope

some are full of a joyous song
a birthday party when I was eight
not mine, I never had them
but a close friend's

we laughed so hard
I spit chili beans all across the table
we all laughed, except Kim's mom

the dance I had with the prettiest girl
in my eight grade class
I felt so peaceful inside
Joy of Heaven filled my soul
with this angel

trudging through the snow
pushing my bike
laden with newspapers
the temperature dipped to thirty below
my gloves were full of holes
my fingers froze

Norway in the depths of winter
slumped shoulders, bowed head
assumed shame of another I bore
shackles that would not let me free
doubts, fears overwhelmed me
where was God? Where was peace
perhaps an unspoken prayer for intercession
perhaps s pleading for torment to cease

these are the things I usually hide
you might see if you dig inside
I wonder what I would see in you
If I chose to take such an internal view

Gnarled Self

loathsome chains
doubt permeates my soul
who am I
do I really even know

each day a search
self truth I long to find
darkness swirls
clouds my fractured mind

I look within
through broken mirror see
my gnarled self
roots of a mutated tree

I probe darkness
to discover a simple truth
path's I've followed, deviated
from a once promising youth

my broken body
with no wings with which to fly
my search for truth
goes beyond the day I die

pluck treasured fruit
courage, to take a hopeful bite
filled with seeds of love
light, to guide my inner sight

my humble prayer
solemn oaths I will not forsake
pursuit of self truth
only path left for me to take

Foment

what does our torment foment
within our tortured minds
doubts and fears so easily beset us
must we really question self
put our motives to the test
fear the shadow regions of thought
avoid dark corners of emotional neglect
Whose visage do we see,
when eyes turn inward to gaze at our reflections?
Our mirrored souls?
Do we recognize what we see?
Is it a stranger? Is it truth?
would we recognize truth if we encountered it
on our dusty path to oblivion?

stir the cauldron of fiery passion
stir up turmoil in your soul with desire
ferment virgin juices, distill virtue
if truth is embraced, will a mighty change of heart ensue?
no longer blinded by falsehoods
as when a pond settles after being disturbed
there are many temptations
there is an over abundance of lies
rain pours a copious amount of painful tears
agitate tortured flood waters
scattering bits and pieces of shattered self along a floodplain
unable to put the pieces together
like a smashed egg that rolls off a wall onto rocks below
the only one who will lick it up is a feral cat or maybe a dog
none want dirt mixed in with their omelette

there are many who dwell in blindness surrounded by reality
choose to be pure in heart instead filled with virtue and love
turn inward to find healing for a desiccated heart
by receiving God's image in our countenances
illuminated within by borrowed light like a moon
realize our divine potential, as eternity reveals
embrace inner truth, don't let others rob us of self

society covers white snow with soot
stirred together it foments something vile
it becomes blackened, no longer pure, filthy
when it melts, you won't even be able to drink it
it is poison to the body and soul
who can remove cinders from snow?
when blackened it remains vile and undrinkable
technology might try to distill pure waters from its impurity
but its sweetness is lost forever, can it ever be pristine again
only a parched tongue would imbibe

peace of soul allows muddy waters to settle
so we might sip sweet, healing waters of light and truth
to purify our hearts, and sanctify our souls
entreat the heavens by virtue of pure and perfect love
silent words inward spoken, as by the gentle cooing of a dove
inspiration etches its answer on the fabric of our souls
with broken hearts and contrite spirits we seek celestial abodes

Drop

on a Polynesian island
a young man
stands on the beach
gazes out across a vast ocean
wonders what mysteries lie beyond
who is he really?
can he really be no more than
a drop in this ocean
which lies at his bare feet?
think of all the drops of water
his tiny drop will touch
when it falls into this ocean
one drop means nothing
to such an immensity
when swallowed up
surrounded by so many
it easily disappears
as if it were as much of nothing
as existence before the Big Bang

courage of a young man
who ventures forth
means more than
a lonely drop
lost in the ocean of life
consider all the lives
touched and blessed
with love and service
by one life well lived
one life well given
completely given
with nothing left on the table
no legendary saint here

just a mere mortal man
a humble son of Tonga
or maybe a true saint
for these latter days

cast a drop into the cosmic ocean
What really is the effect?
cast a charitable heart among mankind
rain falls upon parched ground
dearth turns into life
life achieves meaning

Doubting Disease

I doubt the sanity of my mind sometimes
can these divergent thoughts make up my whole
questions appear and grow near unto torment
my frontal lobes burn with inner concern
pressure on the synapses to melt and fuse
confuse with rebellious contemplations
which go against my personality's predilection
towards what? Sanity? Can such exist in me?
my stolid appearance of sanity belies inner reality
I am like muddy waters stirred up by a stick
What will be left when silt settles?
if I knew, I might hide from your microscopic inspections
put me under a magnifying glass you burn off my wings
with intense rays of noon day sun like lasers burn
off wings of a blue-tailed butterfly, so intense with such nonsense
point the laser at my diseased mind so full of doubt
of who I ought to be, of who you are to me
questions of reality torment me, open your eyes to see
I am my own reality, not what you think I should be
not even what you feel you see when you gaze at doubt filled me
I look within to cast poison from my soul, to cleanse the doubtful me
feels so nice to be squeaky clean inside, purification of tormented soul
sweet as mountain meadow flowers cleansed after healing rains descend
if tears were rain maybe my tears could drive torrential doubts away

guilt, stone cold guilt, raw and hard
blinded by guilt because he looked back
because he touched her sweetness
her purity, pure as a fluffy newborn chick
innocent in all its aspects, lovely and vibrant

he was not innocent, when he touched her fluff
her purity, overwhelmed by his carnal desires
like a hungry wolf who sought to devour
the yellow chick, and left her soul in ruins
his soul in ruins, spirit-sick from defilement

he could not live with the burden of his lust
he could only be sated by her, by stealing her
by touching her, by feasting upon her purity
by defiling all that was virtuous in her
now he must die, guilt condemned him

the red Mustang convertible crashed through trees
like rolling thunder, an avalanche shredding limbs
dismembering oaks, aspens, firs, and spruces
leaving a wreckage of vegetation reflecting
the wreckage of a tortured, lustful heart

he had been told, "Don't look back!" too late!
a legend of Lot, Sodom and Gomorrah, remembered
"Don't look back!" The warning unheeded by Lot's wife
a body turned to salt, his heart turned to stone
descended into darkness now, his empty cave a grave

his thoughts turned to her, the besmirched one
he thought it was love's desire, turned putrid now
like a foul smelling swamp, when mists rise
mists obscure the sun, obscure sight, inner sight
lust and carnal desire obscure love's true view

the cherry red Mustang slammed into boulders
its engine pushed hard into the dashboard
the dashboard pushed the steering wheel
into his chest, crushing him, heart still beat
airbag malfunctioned, salvation lost

he looked up to feel the conflagration
consume his flesh, charred flesh, scent of burnt hair
roasted ribs, broken and shattered, roasted and toasted
a spark found the gas line, the gas line the tank
explosion, a miniature supernova, death merciful, pain
gone?

could such a one ever dwell in heaven?
or burn in eternal hell? who dares judge?
his last memory was the feel of her beneath him
when he ripped her dress, tore her heart, felt her...
the last voice he heard, the echo of her cry for mercy

he showed no mercy, gave himself none
would she judge him? when he had condemned himself?
Who can tell? Who would tell? Who would be so bold?
What truly happened when he chose his private hell?
he could not exercise his demons, forever within him
dwell

he died to possess her secrets, which were only hers to
give
he killed himself inside, so he chose never again to live
desire possessed his soul, he could no longer control
a way to protect the one he loved, his ultimate desire
was to choose this suicide, a physical sacrifice by fire
Don't look back

Don't Look Back

guilt, stone cold guilt, raw and hard
blinded by guilt because he looked back
because he touched her sweetness
her purity, pure as a fluffy newborn chick
innocent in all its aspects, lovely and vibrant

he was not innocent, when he touched her fluff
her purity, overwhelmed by his carnal desires
like a hungry wolf who sought to devour
the yellow chick, and left her soul in ruins
his soul in ruins, spirit-sick from defilement

he could not live with the burden of his lust
he could only be sated by her, by stealing her
by touching her, by feasting upon her purity
by defiling all that was virtuous in her
now he must die, guilt condemned him

the red Mustang convertible crashed through trees like
rolling thunder, an avalanche shredding limbs
dismembering oaks, aspens, firs, and spruces leaving a
wreckage of vegetation reflecting
the wreckage of a tortured, lustful heart

he had been told, "Don't look back!" too late!
a legend of Lot, Sodom and Gomorrah, remembered "Don't
look back!" The warning unheeded by Lot's wife

a body turned to salt, his heart turned to stone descended
into darkness now, his empty cave a grave

his thoughts turned to her, the besmirched one
he thought it was love's desire, turned putrid now
like a foul smelling swamp, when mists rise
mists obscure the sun, obscure sight, inner sight
lust and carnal desire obscure love's true view
the cherry red Mustang slammed into boulders
its engine pushed hard into the dashboard
the dashboard pushed the steering wheel
into his chest, crushing him, heart still beat
airbag malfunctioned, salvation lost

he looked up to feel the conflagration
consume his flesh, charred flesh, scent of burnt hair roasted
ribs, broken and shattered, roasted and toasted a spark found
the gas line, the gas line the tank
explosion, a miniature supernova, death merciful, pain gone?

could such a one ever dwell in heaven?
or burn in eternal hell? who dares judge?
his last memory was the feel of her beneath him
when he ripped her dress, tore her heart, felt her...
the last voice he heard, the echo of her cry for mercy

he showed no mercy, gave himself none
would she judge him? when he had condemned himself?
Who can tell? Who would tell? Who would be so bold?
What truly happened when he chose his private hell?
he could not exercise his demons, forever within him dwell

he died to possess her secrets, which were only hers to give he
killed himself inside, so he chose never again to live desire
possessed his soul, he could no longer control
a way to protect the one he loved, his ultimate desire
was to choose this suicide, a physical sacrifice by fire

Burdens

burdens of my mind weigh as heavily as oceans pounding a barrier reef
chains of a past gone awry, void of wisdom from ancient sages
a plethora of mistakes and misdeeds scattered along my path
I walk along a shore covered in refuse, frustrated with existence
dark wrathful clouds follow me as if I am their only friend

Gnarled

gnarled, like a twisted piece of driftwood cast adrift
scattered along a river of corporeal temptations and desires
caught in a logjam of emotions, misshapen by passionate lies
unable to find release, unable to break free from chains of doubt
lost in mists of darkness, unable to see beauty within our own imperfections

Burrito Blanket

I don't know how to reach out with my mind
to drive the aching from your soul
comfort your sorrowing heart, so full of loss
my arms won't reach you to hold you in firm embrace
I cannot drive dreaded disease from your body
I am helpless to act on your behalf save for a simple
prayer of hope
heaven sent on bended knees, to God, on your behalf
wrapped in love for comfort, like you wrapped in your
burrito blanket

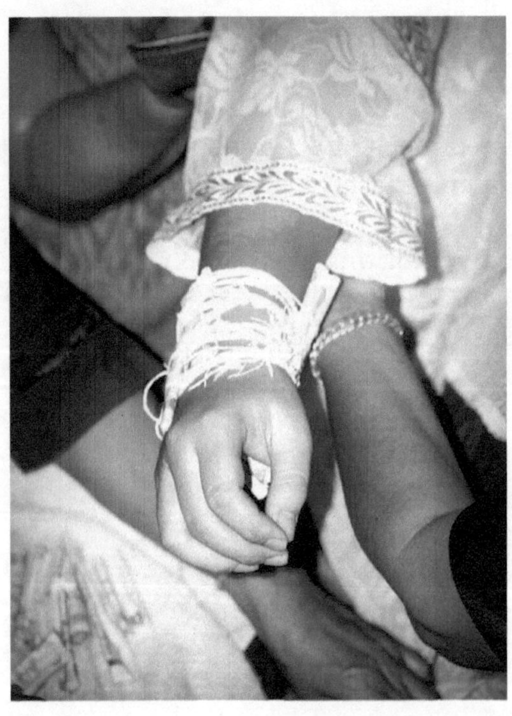

Beauty Within

he had made her feel ugly within
with his most treacherous sin
who is to judge what beauty should be
a voluptuous chest, or a tiny bumble bee

the beaver spoke her silent truth
into her tortured mind
words of comfort and wisdom
to sooth, like cool spring waters
sooth weary, hot feet
that have wandered far
beneath the scorching heat
of the searing west desert sun
a cool spring to fill a beaver pond with hope

"Can there be ugliness without
when there exists such beauty within?"

the eyes that gazed across the shimmering pond
to where the beaver lodge sat crafted
with meticulous care and constant effort
stick by stick, mud pack by mud pack
eyes turned outward could now be turned in
to gaze upon the inner virtuous truth
the gentle maiden sought to know
mirrored on her soul, mirrors of eternity
her soul so naïve and tender
so delicate and refined
as tender as the tan skinned mother roe
who gently nudges her spotted fawn
In forest thicket, shielded from predatory eyes

so now, the gentle maiden's true nature
shielded from the carnal blindness
of the one who should have clearly seen
her beauty within as it should have been
his ultimate destiny, her only truth
she now knew! She knew!
what could not with earthly eyes be seen

Love and Loss

Love Lines

my darling
lying by my side
together to explore and nothing to hide
we discover each other in our familiar parts
fused in this union forever in our hearts

I've never taken the chance to explore inside your cave
it's not that I'm a coward or even that I'm not brave
I'm terrified of what in you I might find
what treasures lurk within the cave that is your mind

let me speak words so sweet
words to knock you off your feet
let me taste your flesh divine
drunken with love's finest wine

to my lady, my true love
given by God's grace above
sealed to me here in my heart
forever mine, to never part

the door is closed the party over it's time to say goodbye
my love is that a tear drop I spy in your eye
bid me to spend this night with you
I will share my love ever true

By the Shore

What did I do to us?
Where did I go wrong?
Was it the story that I told you?
Was it the way I sang my life's song?

you are beyond my reach
rejected and dejected am I
What happened to our true love?
Did it melt into the sky?

sitting here on the lake shore
thoughts of you fill my mind
I didn't mean to abuse our love
I didn't mean to seem unkind

The Lake

sun sparkles on its surface
I sit and think of you
sparse clouds overhead
mostly the sky is blue

canoes and rafts ply upon waters
disturbing it in their wake
fish break the surface
here on Tibble Fork lake

children's voices fill the background
breeze so cool and sweet
I sit here on the dirt shore
swallowed in darkness of defeat

pine trees grow straight and tall
hollows are full of green grass
I didn't mean to offend sensibilities
when my life's story you found crass

reflected on this lake are pine trees
grow to the sky, get so tall
reflected in my tear stained eyes
are the reasons for my fall

my fall from your grace came so quick
my shattered vessel I sit and view
I am vulnerable, let my guard down
Easy prey for the likes of you

Pain in My Brain

there is a pain in my brain
left by your absence
this empty space
like a wind blown desert
when in days long past
you stood by my side
you were with me then
filled my lonely days
took away my pain
treasured our love
spoke kind words
to my troubled heart

you have been blown away
like dust before
driving desert winds
as I feel wind blow
I feel your love blow through me
I know it is you
who once filled my soul
with joyous laughter
please, take away my empty pain
fill my heart with hope
like your sweet fragrance once filled my senses
left your fingerprints upon my life

you are no longer here
your essence filled me way back when
my only hope was our resurrected love
which left me no longer spirit dead
intense pain in my brain lingers to torment me
if you, like an analgesic, were near
to ease torments of lonely nights

my pain would dissipate
like raindrops on flower petals
when sun peaks between storm clouds
to cascades down to touch green earth
so let your love descend upon me

my darling, are you even here
can I even hope to wonder
if though I don't see you
it is possible you are still near
as I see strong winds
blow tree branches
to know its true effect
can my memory of your essence
blow in corners of my mind
stirring up dust
to scatter upon my soul
the way stardust
is scattered through the cosmos
so I can feel your love
to ease my suffering
take away my deepest pain
fill the empty space
which once held you
you encircled in my arms
know the sweet reality of our love again
I will cross the veil to hold you close
imbibe your sweetness
drive severe pain from my brain
make me one with you again

In Love With You

I am in love with the idea of holding you in the night
someone so kind and gentle, pure to rescue me from this blight
a loveless life, my tormented lot
you the joy in spring I have always sought

who are we really when we gaze into each other's eyes
do you feel my passion as you see my tear drops cry
do you know where this tortured soul has been
can you accept me and not call my love a sin

can you really love me for who I choose to be
a ship lost upon life's tumultuous sea
will you guide me safely back to your heart's shore
please hold me close and make love to me once more

are you a dream, or a sweet fantasy or two
when I awaken, will I be left lonely and blue
are you real, or just a figment of my mind
tell me the truth, but with your truth be kind

my love for you is endless and has no bound
this dream of you where my greatest joy is found
to lie next to you and feel your naked body near
to speak sweet softness and have you whisper dear

I am in love with the idea of you whispering my name
lost in your arms as you ignite another flame
the very hope that my contemplation must be true
the dearest contemplation to me is my love realized in you

so come to me to love and feast upon our love tonight
rescue me from loneliness with your divine light
explore flesh entangled in arms eternally
consummate our love on the crystal sea

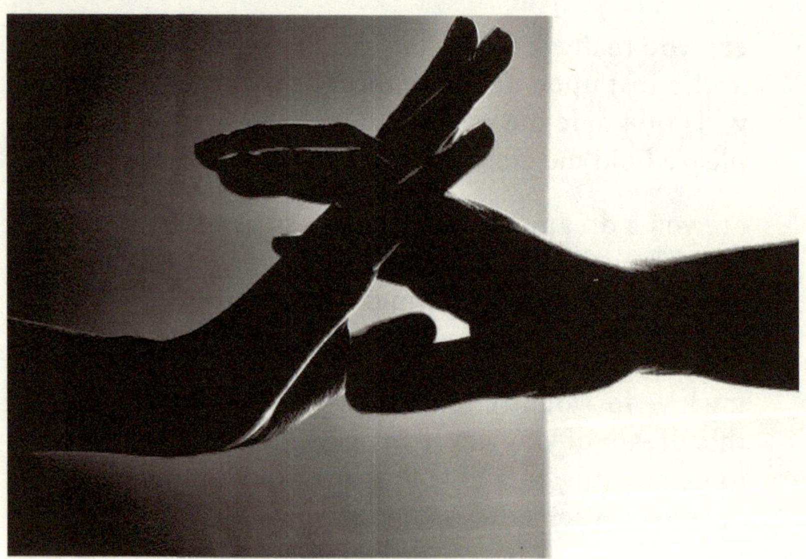

Thoughts of A Friend

you are my friend
but you make me weak in the knees
you are my friend
but you make my tongue freeze
Why do I have to feel this way
Why do you stir sweet longings in my heart
Why can't I just accept your friendship
savor it, and enjoy it without this taint
which Comes from a sordid mind and the stiffness
of my boyish cock between my legs
what vile thoughts fill my mind
when I hear your gentle poetic words
which fall like rain upon my pain
And leaves a stain on my lonely heart.

dreams of you flow through my mind
what in my dreams will I ever find
shatters my heart, breaks mind
leaves all sordid fantasies behind
my love for you is real as the sun
warms my heart, feels like fun
now washes away with a heavy rain
I'm left alone deep in my pain.
images of you etched upon my heart
deep in my soul, cleaves it apart.

Desire

distance
loneliness
a tattered veil
seeks to cloak my soul
hides the tender regions
of my heart from you
and the flames you stir
in the boiling cauldron
of my passionate desires.

Fear

fear is to gaze into the dark unknown without hope
like entering a dark cave not knowing, full of dread
enter by faith, with hope to find the wondrous instead
the greatest fear is to lose something cherished
love is the most precious gift anyone can possess
too often taken for granted, love is so easily discarded
fear of losing love can be one of life's great pains
as painful as swallowing a giant granite boulder
can such a thing be possible? If piece by piece?
yet in the midst of love shared with the treasured one
is losing their love ever a consideration?
yet in the blink of an eye love is gone forever
no explanation ever really given, just gone
like an arctic blast during mid-spring freezes,
destructive all of summer's harvest gone,
so unpredictable, yet obliterates life
so is love when the beloved abandons so unpredictably
leaves you dead inside, your hopes and dreams
obliterated
it would be less painful to swallow the granite boulder
instead loneliness descends like a cold, dark winter's
hell

is there truly any reason to fear the loss of love?
It will happen, if it happens, too many who claim to
love are fickle
fear blinds us to reality of things, to possibilities
innumerable

to those who have loved and lost, fear is ever present
to deny hope
as you wander into caves of life uncertain of treasures
you might find
fear is ever present, but hope remains, or why wander
in caves?
love, like a cave, is entered with no certainty what you
might find
the pain of loss, or the joy of true and perfect love
is the potential treasure enough to warrant venturing
forth?
or will fear prevent you from entering the dark cave of
love ever again
caves contain dangers, bears and cougars dwell within,
so too demons
caves contain great beauty as well, as in the ancient
art of Lascaux
great treasures of gold and diamonds and jewels exist
therein surely this merits venturing into caves of life
and face whatever hell exists
to gain the great treasures of true and perfect love
which dwell therein
fear is a deterrent, but the hope of love and joy can
conquer fear
hope will be a guiding light, when the darkness of fear
surrounds
it can be easy to lose hope, but have courage, venture
forth instead
or let fear leave you dead inside, nothing of value ever
came easy

the cost of true and perfect love is to face the fear of loss with hope instead

Does She Wait

does she wait upon a distant shore
across the veil of sorrow and tears
sorrow for the lifeless body laid to rest
tears shed for one whose light no longer shines
in my velvet night sky, snuffed out in passing

her light was the brightest we have ever seen
so full of joyous laughter and twinkling eyes
her heart loved so deeply, touched so many
love spread upon the earth to cover all
like cascading rain soothes desert pain

she did not want to go, struggled to survive
promises made are now broken
no choice given, as disease enveloped her whole
tears, so many tears shed then, as now
such deep pain, pierces like a dagger to the heart

each day more empty than the last
an empty chair, a vacant place at the table
memories the only source of solace
hope for the eternities the only peace
robed in white she stands upon a distant shore

a beacon of light to help all to see
true source of her divinity is a guiding light
look to her light, trust in its reality
reality is more than what five senses reveal
spiritual reality is the greatest truth of all

does she wait? does she beckon to us?
feel her presence near with spiritual perception

look within, see with your inner eyes
her image is etched upon your eternal soul
a beacon to our ships on stormed tossed sea

she waits on a distant shore for you
she waits beyond the veil for me
a mother's love is eternal as the night sky
love's embrace always proffered, always welcome
reach out to touch her with your mind

reach out, realize, she waits still, feel her near
she waits for you, she waits for me in the eternities

Dreams

on gossamer wings dreams come to us in our sleep
flitting and floating through the velvet night

intangible, they dissipate like the morning mists
beneath the gaze of the rising sun adorned in splendor

like glass they are shattered into a million pieces
whose shards cut the very soul and make it bleed

they fill the mind and heart with longing and desire
for that which cannot be, yet we reach to embrace them

nebulous like a gas giant, they are beyond our grasp
they haunt us in the depths of the eternal night

Shakespearean verse proclaims them the things of which we are made
mirror images of the mind and heart of what we want life to be

to grasp them is to risk insanity, lost in obsessive desire for an illusion
yet to ignore them is to leave the soul in bondage and depression

beauty arises upon the tongue of dreams that laps up the existence of mortals
who but long for the object of their carnal desire only to be frustrated thereby

wind is more real and more tangible than a dream that cannot be obtained

upon the wind that the birds fly and the boats sail into
the wide horizon

lost on the horizon of wakefulness as the mind clambers
to hold on
to the dream that seems like reality but is fools gold
instead

dreams consume us, fantasies and wishes we can only
hope are real
reach for dreams as if they are the stars, will you crash or
touch the moon?

to dream of love is one of the sweetest of all dreams, the
hope of a tender heart
inevitable loss of love, love is fleeting, is as painful as a
knife to the heart

I dreamed of a life so sweet and a love so real that I could
taste its very essence
I got so close, like a viper it rose up and bit my heart and
nearly poisoned it

to dream is to risk all on foolish endeavors, which will
frustrate the best laid plans
to not dream is to encase the mind and soul and heart in
lead, you may as well be dead

dream on dear one, and in your dreams may you find
hope for a better tomorrow
realize it is a hope born on gossamer wings that will flit
and float away

Desperate Little Girls

desperate Little Girls
raven haired curls
who in the Middle East
foreign in the least
who on their wedding bed
when marriage lusts are fed
may well end up dead
if sheets aren't bloody red
desperate little girls
when their banner unfurls
those faithful ones
under bright suns
let their moon juices flow
into bloody streets go
effervescent and bubbling over
onto green fields of clover
or into bloody shame
no one knows her name
tears shed on padded pillow
like the weeping willow
soaked up by purity's veil
left in her own special hell
wrapped with scarf around head
will white turn blood red
to cover her scarlet weaves
tremble like wind blown leaves
if sheets be white, she be dead
means lover before she's wed

desperate little girl
dagger eyes men hurl
twirling around through dark of night
hear the shrill sound, see the sight

desperate little girl pierced by phallus
different from the west of us
wrapped up in violent ecstasy
watch her suffer and you will see
demon's bloody scream
lover's erotic dream
whose tender flesh thrust in maws
ripped open by hungry claws
drips into pools of pain
falls like crimson rain

tear open her beating heart
rip her soul all apart
let toxic tears flow
so, little girls might grow
shed their womanhood
before the altar of good
blood flows crimson red
she will keep her head
upon the reaper's floor
she suffers shame no more

HEZBOLLAH

"Bola, Bola, Bola, Hezbollah!"
chants Ishmael's liberal sons
Where's your rabid bite
upon the neck of
proud Semitic patriotism
whose steel clad phallus
thrusts into the bleeding heart
of your inner sanctum
Lebanon

"Bola, Bola, Bola, Hezbollah"
Arab Leaguers cheer
Grandmother's with babes in arms
whose lugubrious cries
trampled beneath the treads of
Ruth's steel clad chariots of death
upon the blood red soil
of your verdant mistress
Lebanon.

"Bola, Bola, Bola, Hezbollah"
though Martyr's cheer you on
your children run and flee
from rockets angry glare
leaves ground zero bare
will you ever know a peace so free
from malice, or from strife
within your adopted life
of your step-mother dear
Lebanon.

Silence

I feel silence from across the ocean deep
as heavy as if immersed in salt water
is it meant to bring lonely pain
I thought it as unlikely as the desert rain

Rain upon the desert floor
causes desert flowers to bloom
in brilliant reds and yellows
the sage and salt grass to turn vibrant green

Red as the stain upon the virgin white sheets
proof that virgin love, freely given, once sweet
yellow is the hot sun's lethal rays
which leaves the wanderer parched and thirsty

Thirsty for love you imparted incessantly
now dried up is the the empty well of my heart
where is your sweet artesian well to succor me?
I wander in cold desert, where your sun has set upon my soul

Contention

you attack me
as If your tongue
is a sharpened machete
what do you want to do
split my skull in two
shatter my heart to pieces

your words are like needles
that pierce my flesh
my response leaves me
wallowing in a mire of misery
when we attack each other
when we contend
we are monsters
who rake each other's hearts
with venomous claws
like two grizzlies tear each apart
when aroused in anger
so we tear apart each other
is my heart to be your prey
or will you greet me
with a bear hug of love

contention binds us in pernicious chains
formed of cruel words
let us cast these chains aside
let us speak words soft and sweet
like a piccolo playing a lullaby

to cast aside harshness
join together, one in purpose
cast bitterness aside
become a fountain of healing water
to imbibe nurturing kindness
overflow with tenderness
full of respect and consideration
tied as one in compassion's bond

let us speak words of peace
let us see into each other's hearts
to witness divine truth we find there
it is part of our humanity, which we share
cast unwanted misunderstandings away
as if they are rotten fish that smells foul
let me engage you as my brother, sister
let me know you as my friend
friendship should be sweet
evil words are like poison darts
which distort reality
lead to destruction of our souls
I can learn from you,
you can learn from me
In our union of camaraderie
let's see what we can be
sip from the balm of our friendship
let harsh words of contention find an end

Because I Let You Go

I remember where, and I will always remember when
poetry, messages sent, dreams of long walks in the park
dedications and exclamations of love and ardor made
then
movie lists shared, dreams of quiet kisses in the dark
intimate walks to some day take down a snow-covered
lane
you tenderly would wipe the snow off my cheek
your dreams healed my tortured soul and eased my pain
you made the sun shine when the world seemed bleak
These were dreams we wrote of, from across the miles
the passion was so intense, as we shared our hearts desire
all the fire we once hoped for, as we shared our smiles
in reality we dragged our souls through a murky mire
I loved you more intensely than anything I had ever
known
Your poetry titillated me, desires spoken by my soft lips
the desire for you consumed me, it made my spirit groan
just to hold you in my arms, from your body to take deep
sips

What is the sound of my gentle heart breaking?
my cries as i crumble to the cold floor
What is the taste of my weak knees quaking?
to but kiss you once, kiss you twice, then never more
I bleed through this open wound like a sieve
broken hearts, lives shattered, my tormented soul
wounded deep within my heart, I longed to give
Why did you leave me? Because I let you go

The Bedouin's Mistress Never Sleeps

the Bedouin's mistress never sleeps
from dawn to dusk, again as the moon rises and sets
she is ever vigilant, she is always awake
sometimes she is cruel
at others forgiving
the Bedouin makes love to her
as he explores her secrets
learns her moods and emotions
prospers in her protective arms
gives devotion that exceeds his self-sacrifice
she lies naked before him, glorious in her nubile state

in mid-afternoon, he hides from her scorching sun
he takes refuge in the confines of his goat hair tent
so he and his clan might find shelter from her
conflagration
hot, dry, and dusty is the desert floor
burning with an unquenchable passion
few there be who will venture forth
the brave must be resilient
the Bedouin's mistress is the desert
she never sleeps

the Bedouin's mistress provides sustenance for her lover
shrubs for his goat and sheep herds to nibble
herbs to make his jameed, to mix with yogurt to flavor his
Mansaf
adorned with rice, pine nuts, almonds, and goat for his
food platter
a celebration of life at a marriage or with arrival of guests
here at the mansaf the sacrificial goat head stares at him
with markook shrek as his food mat
dates as his fruit, provide sweetness to his meal

amazing how a mistress so apparently barren provides such plenty
the Bedouin never questions her gifts, he is always filled with gratitude
smell of strong coffee and Turkish tobacco wafts through his tent
his beloved mistress provides a breeze to blow smoke and rich scents
out into the red, mauve, and yellow dykes, inviting guests to dinner

Arabian Oryx, once so plentiful
now nearly extinct, once roasted on his fire
a variety of wildlife roams the forbidden landscape of his mistress
she plays nursemaid to all of her denizens
in her extremes, when it is hot she is deadly
when it rains, she brings a deluge
she sends flash floods in her anger through wadis and siqs
the Bedouin must be wary
his mistress is beautiful, but deadly

the Bedouin honors and reverences his mistress in every way
lest she feels jilted as his lover
nothing can be taken for granted among her sandstone sculptures
she has so much to offer her Bedouin lover
often at a very high price
just as her scorpion daughters can strike at any moment
so this mistress shows no mercy if her lover is indiscreet or disrespectful
she will not be taken for granted, she is made of sandstone, not granite

the scorpion queen kills her mate after she has coupled
so will the Bedouin's mistress, if he is fickle, and proves unworthy
so many dangers lurk behind the next rock outcrop
hazards up the next wadi, or over the next precarious rocky incline

where death stalks, there is also opportunity for life
the Bedouin dwells with his beautiful mistress
survives in the harsh grasp of her love
keeps her secrets always from other men's eyes
cisterns of the desert are her life blood
he is succored on sweetwaters hidden below
only he knows where to find them, only he can be satiated
no greater poetic truth exists
than dwells within the mind of the Bedouin gazing across the landscape
of his mistress' silhouette at sunset
the Bedouin's inner truth comes from his passion for her
she succors him, but she requires exactness
he is ever respectful, reverences her beauty, or perishes

the Bedouin is the poet of the desert
he may not always speak the words
but he always knows his inner truth
truth his own existence is tied to his mistress
each Bedouin carries on his own love affair with her
each Bedouin knows her in his own way
each Bedouin has his own love song to sing only for her

the lone Arabian wolf's howl gives evidence
as does the Fennec fox's cry
the Bedouin's mistress never sleeps
her love surrounds him through all seasons

through all hours of night and day
beneath the silver moon she is ever watchful
the Bedouin slumbers soundly knowing his mistress
will be there to greet him in the hours before dawn
then, when her fire peaks over the eastern horizon
to kiss him with her sunlight
to inspire his soul with love
he sends his prayer heavenward in gratitude for her
the Bedouin's mistress never slumbers
from this, great comfort he can take

For My Love

I dwell in darkness as deep as the eternal abyss

your light does not shine upon me to comfort me

as it once did in the days of our reverie and passion

your love is as faint as a distant siren's song upon a rocky shore

once I splashed joyful in the sea beside your grassy hut

your sun beat down upon me, bright and hot

filled my soul with joy and adulation, with hope

I found comfort in your hut, on a reed mat of your weaving

Now you hide your sun behind the storm clouds of life

which threaten to sweep me into the sea of oblivion

your grassy hut is a shattered ruin, I shiver alone

I am always alone, your love has flown! I am alone

First Kiss

when I first kissed your lips, I found them supple and yielding

you surrendered to my soft caress the way water surrenders to stone

water swallows the stone's hardness in its grasp as it flows by

so you enveloped my heart with your passing

I was bewitched by you that Halloween night, entranced by your vanilla scent

you seemed enthralled by my desire to feast upon your moist lips

to devour your supple, wet tongue so full of the heat of your body's passion

probing, ever probing

When we now kiss, your lips are dry and wooden

as unresponsive as a granite cliff, unable to scale

have the years robbed them of their sweet, supple, vanilla flavor?

has the distance left them void of fire, of frozen flame, of passion, of heat?

Did I break your heart?

or did you shatter mine upon your stone, cold heart?

turned cold and frozen as a winter's morn wrapped in ice

before the morning sun can cast its eye upon the chilled ground

unable to cast my warmth upon your frozen heart

Cold, hard, frozen, unable to yield its balm of forgiveness

or accept my contrite soul, prostrate in deep repentance

just as your lips refuse to release their soft, vanilla flame

Just as water dissolves a stone particle by particle as it flows by

may my passion's heat thaw your inner resolve, and ignite your eternal flame

may the healing balm of love flow over our hearts

like cool soothing waters flows over a parched wound

so our fire may burn as one hot enough to boil our passionate blood

That Which is Immutable (The Crucible)

Definition of *crucible*

1

: a vessel of a very refractory (difficult to fuse, corrode, or draw out) material (such as porcelain) used for melting and calcining a substance that requires a high degree of heat

2

: a severe test

3

: a place or situation in which concentrated forces interact to cause or influence change or development

Wisdom's Path

water follows path of least resistance
flows past stones, over pebbles, dissolves all

a beaver builds a lodge of fallen pines, constructs a dam
glacier fed streams fill the pond where trout and frogs thrive

in the dark of a harvest moon night, leaves change color
an owl turns its head to the sound of a meadow vole

Arabic Oryxes walk single-file along a sandstone outcrop
Arabian wolves watch from a distance, shaded from desert sun

a ghost cat watches from a Himalayan ledge as a bharal feeds
a golden eagle, of the rocky Gobi desert, dives upon a jerboa

in a school in South Florida shots are fired, children die, a nation weeps
Paris bombings shatter lives, innocents are lost, terrorism prevails

mindless threats are thrown like daggers, a competition to destroy earth
where is wisdom's path found? survival of the fittest or destruction of all?

Rain

what kind of rain
falls upon your soul's plane?
is it acidic, so full of pain?
makes you sweat, your heart strain

or does sweet and fertile waters flow
to make green things sprout and grow
inner truths within yourself to know
melt winter snow, to drive away caustic woe

soft falling rain can bring you peace
break off mind's chains to find release
cause vision of Inner self and stability to increase
until torrential rains bring emotional moods in a caprice

rain can bring a deluge to destroy
parched cactus flowers, desert rains enjoy
fields of corn and wheat, irrigation waters employ
cast out a deluge of self-doubt, never allow such to annoy

Poisoned Mind

How do you extract poison from a mind?
How do you make a cold heart sing?
for love to be a cure, it must have a source
it's like there's this little seed
needs to be rooted out, torn out
take a surgical knife and cut deep
or you'll never get it all
you'll never totally be free
poison shackles your mind
doesn't matter if it's source is perversion
or dark reflections of violent tendencies
born of self-loathing, acting out to escape
you never do, you never will
you can't get rid of poison by ingesting more
you can't rid yourself of dark seeds if you feed them
you can't get rid of them by pretending to be Mary
Poppins either
believing in lies only adds darkness, tightens shackles
is there any hope, can you find mercy
only if you are willing to delve deep within your soul can
you know
you have to dig through all your inner baggage, toss it
aside
shatter that dark, vile mirror that won't let you see
delve deep, like probing a dark pool in a hidden cave
there is an inner truth that provides a key
I don't know what it is, maybe no one does
dig for it, pray for it, cast your eyes inward to seek it
maybe it's overgrown with green moss or vines
maybe what you actually need is a hoe, or a machete
if you were in a desert you could use a trowel to dig up
ancient treasure
would you even recognize what it is if you found it?

it seems there are no easy answers, not for vital questions
maybe love isn't such a bad idea after all
can something as beautiful as love come from a poisoned seed?
can all the tears cascading down into gutters like rain
reflect the hurt you've endured, you've caused, all your pain
ever wash away or dislodge the vile seed, a hurricane couldn't do it
what makes you think tears can
feeling sorry for yourself entraps
self-disgust and self-loathing won't help
like sticking a wet finger in an electric socket
you can go to a shrink who might help you heal
until you figure out that what they say is window dressing
you know the truth, you know who you are
you also knew how to mess yourself up
instinctually you know where to find your own cure
within your soul is truth that can grow, a seed of hope
there are opposites in all things
this seed when nurtured grows into a tree
this tree bears fruit, sweet above all other fruits
figure out the metaphorical truth of this fruit, imbibe it
it will cleanse, it will purify, it will makes things whole
that is the only truth I have to proffer
be patient, given time, you will figure the rest out
it won't be easy, you'll need help
guidance from divine sources, inspiration, revelation
some mysteries we never fully understand
suffer long and be kind, endure, have faith, cling to hope
it's within you, find it, virtue will fill you with inner light
you choose which seed to nourish
you determine which seed will grow
there is no destiny, there is only urgency and choice

yet these are the most powerful gifts we are given
walk wisdom's path to find truth, to experience joy

Kiss

kiss fervent lips of my mouth
oh, tortured angel
imbibe succor from my soul
fold your wings around me
draw each breath in
feel my flesh
pressed through you
taste my lips of sin
draw wet well spring from me
rapture for your soul
devour my every passion
only healing you will know

Into My Mind

If I delve deep into my mind what will I find?
What treasures would I uncover so sublime?
Who am I, when all my onion layers are peeled off?
maybe I'm an artichoke with a tasty green heart to consume
Do any of us really know completely who we are?
certainly life is a journey of self-discovery, seen with inner eyes
like entering a cave in hopes there are no grizzly bears within
we hope we don't find any monsters, or past forbidden sins
I am certain we want to view ourselves lovely as a decorated tree
find a treasure of gold and jewels to bedeck our tattered lives
maybe in reality it's a menagerie, or a kaleidoscope of good and ill
when you start to stir yogurt it's white, the fruit below brings forth color
our assumed purity if mixed with self-indulgent lies becomes discolored
most of us want to think the best of who we are, so nurture self-virtue
it's easy to look at another to see a beam, our mote seems so much smaller
but do we scrutinize ourselves to that extreme, not usually it seems
it's scary when we delve into dark secrets of self, take life's book off our shelf
are we prepared for what is found, something ill or quite profound

this inner journey into self we all need, cleanse our inner vessel to proceed
find our source of hope for eternity, so uncover our own true identity

Inner Conflict

twisted lies gnarl minds, distort reality
who am I to question God's veracity
I am nothing, I am nobody
I must humbly seek truth of my inner being
at the altar where covenants are entered into
embroiled in my own war with inner weakness

if weaknesses are to be strengths
I need light from divine guidance
for me to embrace truth and right
cast aside evil which cankers my soul
embrace all things virtuous, lovely, praiseworthy
I must discover my own inner light
which lines the pathway to self-actualization
or is it paths which lead to my damnation?

I can only break chains of death and hell
with virtue and pure, perfect love within
virtue as spiritually powerful
as an act of creation
love as pure as the bond
between a mother and her newborn babe
as perfect as celestial laws moving in concert
Do I even know who God sent me here to be?
Do I know who I am here to love?
surely those most worthy will receive my love
surrounded by hearth and home
Does my heart betray my reality?
Do desires blindly override all?
Do I embrace the covenant path?
to follow it into the eternities
where she waits for me

What is the blessing I am sent here to be?
I only doubt my capacity to love perfectly
I have no capacity to understand
what pure and perfect love even entails
if I show it, or experience it, will I even know?
I do not doubt the existence of divine reality
I doubt my capacity to live God's truths
show faith by obedience to divine laws
faith to take my journey through deserts
to find my own promised land within
to fight for existence, and realize true potential
or be brought low by the sting of self-doubt
a war for truth and lies rages on
inner conflict is just part of my existence

In Your Garden

In your garden, I am the forbidden fruit
If you partake of me, you will find me forever sweet
The knowledge you discover, encapsulated in my seed
Wrapped within the fleshy parts you've devoured
Is my life's truth, my greatest truth is love
My greatest love is you
So take me and eat to fill your hunger
As the forbidden fruit of your garden

In your garden, I am the black and orange monarch butterfly
Who floats and dances amongst the petals of your flowers
I seek love's nectar, your delectable, delicious nectar
I unroll my long tongue and dip it deep inside you to imbibe
I drink deep your elixir of love from between your spread petals
Then I dart about spreading this pollen of life and love
Until I have touched each flower
Dipped my tongue into each blossom
Lapped up the sweet nectar of each anther
Deposited my essence on the stigma of each pistil
To fertilize your heart with my love so it might grow

In your garden, I am the sun and the rain
I make your precious flowers grow
When my radiant, yellow head rises at dawn
You raise your blossoms to receive my light and warmth
To follow me on my journey through the sky
Accept my precious gift of light, don't question why
I am the rain to descend upon your soul
I quench your parched thirst
I leave a raindrop on the petals of each blossom

Like teardrops of heaven
Sent to heal your lonely heart
Then as my sun rays break through grey clouds of despair
My sunlight cascades down upon your garden
So you will know I'm always there
When I set upon far western horizon
And my golden light turns red
I send the moon, my reflected light
To watch over your garden as it sleeps
How lovely are your blossoms under pale moonlight
As the moon's silver essence kisses each petal in your garden

In Desert

in desert I wander
in desert I find peace
in desert of my affliction I find truth
I learn who I ought to be
Who ought I to be?
come into my desert and wander
come into my desert to see

Zeus gazes in situ through vacant eyes
I look across the valley at empty tombs
millennia ago camel caravans plied this desert
bearing a wealth of spice cargo
wealth flowed through this ancient city
blossomed like a rose in the desert
until Trajan's phalanxes marched forth to end it all
earthquakes buried temples and palaces
in the desert where I stood, in the desert of my youth

today I stand on precipice of old age
in desert of my life I am consumed by sand
love does not rain upon me here
as dry as the desert's empty sky, temperatures rise
except in underground cisterns buried deep inside
only from these sources can I imbibe

in the desert a Bedouin family wanders
uncertain of difficulties faced moment by moment, day to day
they dwell on the edge of existence in tents for shade
each day a search for a source for water to sustain
if a well or cistern is empty, they must find another or perish

no room for any error, no more chances if they get it wrong
such is a life without love, love to comfort
love to nurture, in the desert of my pain
scorched by the rising sun, dry without love's easing rain
tribes seek for food, their constant need, to hunt, to gather
Arabian oryx makes a sacrifice to help survive another day
I seek for love to fill my aching need, I search in vain

I seek living waters to heal in the desert of my life
I seek an oasis for my soul to find peace, to find you

sits a woman waiting patiently by a well, comes a stranger
her humble offer of water for his thirst, he drinks
he offers her so much more instead, his living waters
she may never thirst again, eases inner torment of life's pain

I ascend into the mountains in the midst of my desert
to get a witness, a vision of my eternal truth
like Moses ascended into Sinai, a burning bush, the hand of God
in this desert of my soul all things sacred, all things divine
I seek answers to questions that do beset me
torment me like scorpion stings seek to pierce my heart
Where is my burning bush to teach me?
Where is the tablet for the hand of God on which to write?
God write it on the tablet of my soul, living words of my existence

healing words of veracity to descend upon my parched soul

here in desert of my life I am left to wander
in desert of my life I seek myself
in desert of my life I thirst to understand grim reality
to fight for existence, only the fittest survive
come wander in my desert with me
together we'll find our path to inner beauty
together we'll discover our inner truth

In My Nexus of Pain...

in my nexus of pain I find healing
quench eternal flame

in my nexus of pain I find release
shatter prolific chains

in my nexus of pain I find humanity
cleanse by torrential rain

in my nexus of pain I find humility
venerate on contrite knees

in my nexus of pain I find virtue
contemplate in purity

in my nexus of pain I find salvation
nailed through hands and feet

in my nexus of pain I find compassion
imbibe cistern waters sweet

in my nexus of pain I find eternity
repent, paths of darkness forsake

in my nexus of pain...

In Desert

in desert find beauty brutal as a black cobra
in desert find death dogged as a dromedary camel
in desert find wandering wearisome as white bursage
in desert find prayer providential as a prophecy
in desert find cisterns crisp as a caracal's cry
in desert find humility halcyon as a Hajj
in desert find survival savage as a scorpion
in desert find freedom feral as a Fennec Fox
in desert find oracles overflowing as an oasis
in desert find burning bushes beneficent as a barrel
cactus
in desert find sacrifice sacred as a scarab
in desert find revelation radiant as Rhea
in desert find truth triumphant as a thunderbird
in desert find salvation solitary as a sand cat
in desert find seclusion secret as a skink
in desert find God glorious as a golden eagle

Hurricane

Hurricane if a hurricane
comes at you
with all its
terrifying
power to
destroy
breathe it in
let it consume you
become the hurricane
with your own power
to employ
I am the Hurricane
who will consume you
together we as one
are hurricanes
with power
of passion
for existence
to deploy

Hole

there is a hole in my heart
cast in your line to reel in
my inner truth
if you do
please let me know
what you discover
I don't know who the hell I am
besides, I'd like a second opinion

I must be wary of whom
I allow this privilege
there are many jackals
lurking in the tall brush

Babylon

children of Babylon
horrors of earth
spiritual corpses
in need of rebirth

suck life and hope
out of penitent souls
chop down tree of life
wherever it grows

spread mayhem like seeds
strewn upon fertile ground
grow evil like weeds
choked without a sound

darkness dispersed
with a wind blown hand
blind eyes with hatred
break minds cross our land

our only shield
virtue of charity
distilled upon souls
reveals self verity

full of a baleful sound
to bring self clarity
to fit snug as a glove
for all eternity

To Know God's Mind

to know the mind of God what would it take
reach beyond the spirit realm, body forsake
know what path leads to pure felicity
know all spiritual truth only God can see
to gaze into the depths of eternity
for creation be filled with only charity
realize purpose of each molecule at a glance
rejoice to watch beauty in its cosmic dance
I am not God, more like a gnat or a flea
or maybe I'm an acorn fallen from God's tree
full of hope and all wondrous possibility
I wonder what in the end I really shall be

Eternal Flame

eternal flame burns bright red
to consume hearts of passion
moths are so attracted
to be consumed in a flame
hot is the passion
which ignites
within the sacred cauldron
of the eternal flame
love burns bright red
only to turn soft blue
as compassion is born
of red hot passion
compassion is love
forever it will endure
transformation
only occurs
within the cauldron
of the eternal flame
one cannot really love
unless the spark of passion
Is consumed by the beauty
of compassion
like the blue tailed butterfly
breaking forth from its cocoon

Echoes of Petra Revealed

look out through rose colored eyes
upon the desert floor, bone dry
weary of the heat, the heat
weary of the heat
hanging in the still air
like a ghostly presence
shimmering mirages
in this vast distance
here where colonnaded streets, where streets
here where colonnaded streets
winged temples stood
civilizations sleep, they sleep
civilizations sleep
earthquake strewn rubble all around
litters the face of this ancient ground, this ground
litters the face of this ancient ground
silent sentinels stand
in rose colored cliffs
carved by the ancients
left to drift
into the sands of time
lost in the shimmering heat, the heat
lost in the shimmering heat
forgotten and forsaken
until uncovered by a trowel
ancient secrets revealed
vibrant cultures now stilled, now stilled
vibrant cultures now stilled
echoes of the past, uncovered at last
echoes of the past

Broken Heart

sometimes I am in such torment I fear I will go insane
evil from the past comes to haunt me
I try to cast it off, but it won't let go
like something spiritual made of adhesive
even like being stuck in a tar pit
I don't want to end up like a dinosaur
I am tortured by my mind's intense pain
Like a searing hot brand is scorching my mind
all I seek is comfort, all I desire is release
my faith is made of the fabric of my spiritual experience
when I was fifteen I received a witness
I read a holy book, and received a witness, a testimony
my weaknesses keep me from realizing potential
only God truly knows what that is, who I am
but I hope it's more than I have been
I think many who seek spiritual reality might agree
we seek a manifestation, we desire divine truth
too many mistakes made to haunt my waking moments
torment me at night as I toss and turn in agony
only God can give me release, only God can heal my soul
it isn't a freebie, there are no such things
even the air we breath requires lungs that put forth effort
what does God require? Everything!
If we give all we are to God, he provides all spiritual
needs
I subject my selfish will to God, he feeds me spiritually
Christ submitted his will to the Father
How can I expect to do any less?
if in this world I only find sorrow
in the eternities I will know peace
so break my stony heart to let poison flow free
I must be cleansed of evil contemplations

my inner vessel purified, pieces sealed together, soul sanctified
my contrite spirit demonstrates God's will be done
if my path is beset with tribulations, I know God walks with me
when I am blind and lost in mists of darkness
only through God's eyes can I see
God break the stony vessel of my heart
so in healing I might know peace
and so, not fall to pieces

Chains Which Bind

chains bind minds and souls
poisonous thoughts bring chains
like being trapped
in spiritual quicksand
stuck to a tar baby
like Br'er Rabbit
caught and ensnared
by wily foxes
mind entrapped in a quagmire
guilt ensues to bind the soul
extreme struggle
buries one deeper
cast pernicious thoughts
from tormented mind
embrace virtue instead
spiritual power breaks chains
pure thought flows
dissolves chains
like debris washed away
by healing rain
quenches tortured souls

society's opinion brings chains
society labels us
labels bind our souls
prevents self-actualization
controls with shame
accept lies of society
which will bind you down
hold you back
blind you to your true self
rob you of your potential
drowning in a morass of false opinion

pure and perfect love
breaks chains and heals hearts
a mother's touch is a balm
sweet tonic for souls
to gaze into a broken heart
feel deep empathy
mother's touch heals
wipes away a tear
comforts with a soft embrace
breaks chains of sorrow
comforts like a warm blanket
made of compassion and acceptance

lusts of the flesh bring pains from chains
toxic love binds the heart down
false to a true manifestation of love
romance is a fleeting feeling
emotions deeply felt
dissipate like dew from off rose petals
when sunlight casts its gaze
upon intertwined hearts
to reveal lack in the beloved
to see glaring weaknesses
so obscured by the reverie
of primal desire
so blocked out by
initial misconceptions
what was assumed real is a lie

lusts blind the mind
carnal desire binds the soul
to truly know the beloved
peeling off layers
like peeling an artichoke

to retrieve the sweet heart
buried deep within
layers of leaves tossed aside
to observe truth and reality
true love will pierce layers
to find true value in what is sought

flaws do not denigrate
flaws accentuate
reality is not ugly
unless evil is at its core
evil seeks to hide deep
from sunlight of self-truth
when beauty of reality is revealed
love more clearly sees

true love embraces the whole
true love can only grow
when ebbing romance
reveals the whole, flaws and all
only by loving with pure and perfect love
can reality be embraced and appreciated
for the absolute treasure it is
more valuable than the golden touch of Midas
because it is the golden touch of true love
with power to break chains
power to heal broken hearts
power to purify sullied minds
power to mend tortured souls
healing the very fabric of existence
the way a celestial seamstress artfully mends
a tear in the fabric of space and time

pure and perfect love heals
it comes from hearts and souls of angels

mothers are angels, when they nurture
others nurture with spiritual power to heal
choose to be one who heals
choose to love unconditionally
choose to love with pure and perfect love
to shatter chains all to pieces
with power of a hammer to shatter steel
upon the anvil of your heart
cause a fountain of healing water
to break forth from the fabric of your soul
cover the parched ground with pure and perfect love
when we heal nurture another, when we seek to heal
we find we heal ourselves, and find inner peace
freed from chains
a wellspring of sweet water
bitterness ceases to flow

Chains

chains bind me
drag me down
force me into oblivion
to disappear
transformed into
an existence
so much less than myself
something vile
something I reject
falsehoods
carnal judgements
not born of God
not produced by love

God does not lie
God does not chain
God's laws liberate
mind...
soul...
love...
lies are chains
labels foisted on us by society
or assumed upon ourselves
because we lack understanding
we lack self-love
we lack inner truth

divine truth liberates
divine truth flows from
a fountain to heal inner self
filled with perfect love
self-love defines inner truth
not forced from others

rather through loving influence
choice breaks chains
If based on inner truth
born from self-love and virtue
lies bind us to our carnal nature
truth liberates
truth purifies
truth is a pathway to love

no poison to the soul
ever came out of the mouth of God
not from society's God
reflective of its self
rather, the one God who creates
truth to exist in the minds and souls
of those who break chains
of decadence and perversion
only virtue and perfect love
will ever break vile chains
to let souls live free again
in spiritual resurrection of self

life is a journey to self
take your journey courageously
to find endless joy
be wary the pitfalls and chains of lies
of those who lie in wait to deceive
decide your own path
determine which wind
will catch your sails
seek guidance from the God
who speaks in silent whispers to your soul
your receptacle of truth and love
your only source of inner truth
is your light of love and virtue within

Angelic Presence

when God once saw an awful dearth
of angelic presence upon green earth
He thought to turn it all around
with the sweetest smile He ever found
you became God's angel dear
to brighten lives as they drew near
shine forth through dark of night
God's angel full of brightest light

Angel of Death

I am the Angel of Death
I kill the old
plow it under
deep into clay soil
turns to mud when it rains
slick and gooey like peanut butter
only tastes like dirt, tastes like...
you feel growth pains
as I usher in the new, growth hurts
I plow under preconceptions
delusions of the mind
lies told to invest the heart in muck
I plow under chaotic behavior
you want to do as you please
void of all restrictions
even God is governed by
His own divine laws
God can choose to do anything
He chooses wisdom's path
He chooses to be God
to obey His own divine laws
to choose any other path

would dethrone Him
all beings have agency
misuse leads to consequences
betrays the divine within
I plow under the false concept
the lie that freedom should rule unchecked
consequences are tied
to the laws of the universe
I plant the seeds of order, cultivate truth
planted into your newly plowed garden
resist change and you will be plowed under
adaptability is always your only recourse
in this universe of wave functions
which lead to Eigenvalues
probability governs all
God does indeed roll dice
the crapshoot of change determines reality
adapt or perish is an axiom
be planted, and grow, or be plowed under
Choose! Decide!
choice will always be possible
when the Angel of Death comes reaping
I am the Angel of Death
I am the God of change

Catharsis-
healing and release

Catharsis refers to the purification and purgation of emotions—particularly pity and fear—through art or any extreme change in emotion that results in renewal and restoration.

Wikipedia

Spire

spire, across from which
trumpeting angel stands
trumpet forth eternal truth
onion shaped minaret
call echos to God
invitation to prayer
to seek shared truth
stab a spire through your heart
what good will it do
handle and see
the holes in hands and feet
feel the hole in the side
spire was a spear
Mohammed heard the words
“Recite”, and spoke truth
united Arab tribes
Quran’s truth spread
with this truth many bled
so many dead
one truth to unite all
one name to end bloodshed
yet variation on a tune
leaves division
like a deep gash in the earth
speak your inner truth
are these variations on a theme
really all that different
if Mohammad’s feet
were ever bloodied in journey
surely they bleed still
if Christ’s wounds bled once
surely they bleed still
what about the pastoral lamb

surely it bleeds still
with so much bleeding
too many centuries drenched in blood
surely it is time to end bloodletting
time to end war of faith
time to find doves of peace
time to heal spiritual wounds
time to see the minaret and spire
point to the same God
let his love heal
torn and tattered nations
our true enemies are
hatred, avarice and greed
these feed upon
humble souls of men
who prostrate on bended knees
worship the same God
no matter what name is used
it's all the same
it's all the same
no matter God's name
it's all the same

do you tire
of my spire
with an Angel
on top
to see him pirouette
on your lofty minaret
I would never forget
names are labels
we all give
you worship Allah
there is none but he
I worship Jesus

who wandered Galilee
Jehovah brings
Wailing Wall prayers
Buddha chants
from lofty temples
echo between
Himalayan peaks
It's all the same
no matter what his name
God's still the same
I'm right
You're wrong
we throw epithets
in disgrace
but the thorn crested
Christ's forehead
blood runs down
his cheek and chin
to release mankind
in resurrection
from carnal sin
His pure and perfect love
Muslims fought
For Mohammed
no crucifixion
adorned his humble head
so much blood thereby shed
by Muslims
by Christians
must we really keep score
Israelis took part
do we really need to shed any more
we fight for resources
label it with God's name
God must view it all

and only feel the shame
of abuse of his sacred name
when we only have
ourselves to blame

Gull's Prophecy

lone winged gull
witness mankind's desecration
while scavengers descend
along rotted shore
it doesn't have to be
this desolation by the sea
lone winged gull caws
in prophetic lamentation
follow truth on bended knee
follow the one from Galilee
cries the sage like gull
along man's scavenged shore

Guilt

guilt is an unpleasant burden
reminds me I am imperfect
too many sources to count
it's like all the small sources
come together in a confluence of guilt
like streams and rivers
in the Amazonian river basin
dump water into the mighty amazon
creates a great delta
water carried forth into the Atlantic
a snowflake in the Andes
becomes a part of tons of water
flowing into the Atlantic in great abundance
so to does ever little sin
every mistake and misstep
whether in action or thought or word
lead to my confluence of guilt
the burden is overwhelming
only by sharing this burden
with one who cares
who won't turn away
who won't abandon me
in my moment of pain and need
only by sharing the burden
might I find any salvation
each sin adds weight
breaks my inner vessel a little more
love cannot dwell in a broken vessel
I can only be healed by perfect love

Through God's Eyes

What does God expect? What does man?
What should we call the spiritual gap between?
economists speak of gaps, inflationary, recessionary
children lose baby teeth, leave cute gaps between
minds full of trivia leave empty gaps between two ears
until of course life's jeopardy crowns a champion

to know what God expects we must see as God sees
not an easy task, easier to imagine what people think
God is boundless, infinite, eternal, omnipresent
our feeble minds barely begin to understand the universe we see
yet there are theories, laws of physics that seek to explain what we see
what do we see as we gaze into the mysteries of eternity?
do we see the handprint of God? or do we see a reflection of ourselves?
I doubt we would be able to discern, we too often create god's in our image
rather than seek to understand the God who exists, we worship self
a spiritual gap between humankind and God is infinite and eternal
it is a concept instead of a specific value, it is not a number
it spans the expanse of space and time, and beyond
all things that have ever been, and all things that ever can be
worlds without number, beyond what technology is able to grasp

How then do we come to know the mind of God?

if we listened for God's answer, he might whisper it in our ears
If we approach the throne of God to ask, what would he say?
I don't believe God gives answers to ease conscience
I believe he requires more than mere lip service
I don't believe God responds to insincerity
sackcloth and ashes are required instead
broken hearts, and contrite spirits will certainly help
we are too caught up in self to subject our will to another's
even if that will is God's, the only will that can heal us, help us
unless some tragedy or loss bring us to our knees, to beg please
when life becomes a torment where can we find peace?
Balm of Gilead? A comforter? A suffering God who offers peace?
a suffering God who suffers with us? as well as for us? who understands?

seek within to know your own truth, let God's light guide your way
divine answers only come to the contrite in spirit
look to God and flourish, rely only on self and perish
we can truly see through God's eyes
by seeing within ourselves through his eyes
if you can take this inner journey to self
you might be able to see another through God's eyes, as well
to understand why God cherishes each soul as he does
look through his eyes to see as he sees, to love as he loves
discover why we all have meaning to God
regardless of our station in life, regardless of wealth or stature

we all have meaning, we all have worth
we all have purpose when seen through God's eyes
through God's eyes see beauty rare, beyond compare.
it is unique, it is creation, it is me, it is you, it is us

Gaze Upon the Soul

to look within
to gaze into
the mirror
of your soul
is to gaze
upon the beauty
of your true divine self
you see perfectly
with your inner eye
all the possibilities
that make up you
the gift of inner sight
is precious
for with it you can gaze
into the inner self
of your beloved
with all of their
wondrous possibilities
it is like gazing into
the celestial beauty
of a gaseous nebula
creation of stars occurs
stars are the beginning of possibilities
when you see more clearly
you love more perfectly
you see flaws
true, you see perfection too
you see possibilities
you help them see
through your bond
of perfect love
you are knit as one
so it is when you gaze
into the soul of your beloved

Fountain of Truth

What is truth?
What fountain spews it forth?
Can a bitter fountain bring forth sweet, healing waters?
Can falsehoods save a soul, save society?

being nice can be window dressing for lies
told to preserve emotions, feelings left unhurt
kindness seeks tactfully to speak words of truth
Whose truth? God's truth!
How do we learn this truth?
it might appear to be beyond the corporeal realm
can our finite minds even imagine it
all must learn a pathway to truth
all must find truth's source, our own fountain of truth
which like a sweet artesian spring
provides healing waters from which all can drink
when we find the pathway to God's truth, his fountain of truth
we find the pathway to our own
we learn who we are, who we are meant to be

perversion distorts truth, distorts reality
twists perceptions into pernicious lies
we only see through opaque mirrors
mirrors of eternity shattered, their credibility betrayed
perversion flows from Satan's vile tongue
always false, always evil
Hitler spoke of ubermench
when his only true goal was to destroy mankind
drag society through the gutter of Nazi swill
too many would be leaders do little more
spewing forth their poison like a gusher of toxic waste

break chains of evil, discard vile thoughts
doubts and fears that afflict the soul
cast out spiritual poison
like pulling noxious weeds from their deepest roots
cast it onto the bonfire of veracity
deny selfish intent and self-aggrandizement
be cleansed by the power of the Savior's atonement
open your heart to his love, your mind to his divine words
to be made pure in heart, at one in Zion
afflicted with poison no more

drink from the healing fountain of truth
cleanse the inner vessel, be filled with virtue
full and overflowing with pure and perfect love
enough to heal a world full of suffering and pain
empathetic compassion for those who suffer
healing balm for those who mourn
let your fountain overflow with living waters
from which all who seek truth can imbibe
give freely to all who desire it
or your fountain of truth will turn brackish
blown away over time as dust
like a dried up useless old well
while you experience your own version of hell
covered by your own lies and deception
like maggots covering a rotting carcass
like fountains of truth flow freely instead

Fountain of Truth Revisited

pitfalls of society are snares
like being entrapped in a tar pit
all you do is sink down and down
unless you are thrown a rope for your rescue
Jesus Christ throws such ropes
in his teachings of virtue and compassion
Buddha understood these truths, as did Lao Tzu
assist another on their path to truth
you also help yourself
we succeed best as one

listen to no lies told to destroy you
lies are spiritual poison
Satan is their source
servants of hell are purveyors of perversion
lies flow from their serpentine tongues
forked and malevolent, full of venom
infects those who hear, a pox on the fabric of society

the past is a pitfall sent to haunt us, don't let it
it distracts from what is needful today
too much guilt blinds the mind and scars the soul
forgiveness and spiritual progression are the cures
we can't see the sunrise if our eyes are muddied
by wallowing in self-deprecation and self-pity

too often we feel alone, this is a lie
we are never alone
though surrounded by traps and snares
we won't be alone, unless we choose to be
there is one who always watches
there is one who always waits
a fountain of truth from which all can imbibe

a choice must be made, it is ours to choose

find the pathway to your fountain of truth
take it, don't look back
lest your heart turn to stone
and you become spirit blind
without a heart or eyes to see
surely you wander then in strange paths
to be lost in dark mists as lies
look within to find the trailhead for this journey
the journey to your fountain of truth is only taken therein
find a divine light as your guide

God is the source of all truth
an ultimate fountain of healing waters
good fountains bring forth pure, sweet waters
while bitter fountains bring forth pernicious lies
put no stock in lies, only fools countenance them
society is full of lies, society is poisoned by evil
there must also be good in society, but it wanes
we could not know bitter fruit
if we also did not also eat the sweet
where can we find veracity in a society run amok
where can we find good in a culture out of control
who will provide the brakes before we careen off a cliff
seek pathways that lead to fountains of righteousness
we wage a war against evil, wherever it is found
wars for our very souls, wars against the ills of society
reject falsehoods wherever they exist
pull them out by their vile roots
embrace God's truth instead
such is our only hope to heal society

to be one with the Savior, one with God
you must be one with his purpose

what is his purpose?
find your fountain of truth to drink
only then is your mind open to this truth
know this, when you touch the life of others
you leave a piece of yourself in their souls
there are pieces of others within you
they can be your guiding lights
be wary they are not false lights
the pathway of truth leads to eternal life
it is the pathway to God
pathway paved with faith, hope, charity, and love
follow it with singleness of heart
be guided to find self-truth, to realize potential
it is the pathway to our fountains of eternal truths
whose waters we must imbibe
where we can embrace hope, achieve peace
look within to discover your own fountain of truth
it might lie beneath your life's rubble
dig deep to uncover it, there are no free rides
drink deep and live, or let your soul thirst and die

Evolutionary Mind, Reflections

What is this thing called mind?
neurons firing across synaptic gaps
create a mosaic of poetic images
elicited by neurochemical complexity

creative compulsions engender emotions
flush the cortex with cascading pheromones
ignite desires which feed and feast upon imagination
evolutionary dreams of art filled caves of splendor

When did the first creative spark take flight?
elegantly soaring across the synaptic expanse
like an Andean condor first taking flight
poetry in motion amidst the swirling clouds

consider a mountain peak dusted with snow
let the details etch themselves upon the mind
Fixate! Contemplate! beauty is in the details
poetry is a still life composition of emotions

transition the receptors of the mind to a red rose
capture the texture with your fingertips, velvety soft
aromas enliven and arouse the olfactory senses
mind is filled with thoughts of love and romance

symbolism and similes of a creative muse evolve
through introspection on sensory perceptions
evolution of poetry and art, all creative muses
paralleled by evolution through cognitive expression

Opaque

opaque images
twisted and gnarled
like looking through
a fun house mirror
at selves and others
no truth exists
just false opinion
twisted reality
falsehoods, lies
foisted by
a poisoned society
wrapped in
its own deception
a convolution of reality
like an umbilical torus
perspectives reject divine truth
exist as spiritual poison
to twist the soul
to make the holy
appear deranged
the heart and soul
are divine stomping grounds
society's opinions
create opaque images
within the mind
grotesque and vile
a mutated monstrosity
horrors from a haunted imagination
buy into society's twisted perspectives
you will experience spiritual death
you will no longer see truth
you become spirit blind

you no longer sing songs
of redeeming love
instead you speak words
to your own condemnation
society labels people
not in a good way, not in truth
society tries to force false reality
on its poor denizens who cannot see past
the opaqueness of lies surrounding them
so we become imprisoned in chains
labels are pernicious chains
believe in them, they enslave you
break off label's chains, cast your bonds to the floor
shed the unwanted cloak of opinion
define yourself by looking within
align your mind with your own divinity
seek to find God from within, to know truth
reality will always be opaque
unless you see with God's eyes
see as God sees
know as God knows
love as God loves
embrace spiritual reality
uncover inner truth
realize this is the only truth that exists
God is the wellspring of all truth
God is the source of all good things
a sweet artesian spring from which to drink
if you don't believe in the existence of God
where are you?
you cannot find truth
unless you know it's source
there is a fountain of living waters
partake of it to cleanse your tortured soul
bitter fountains bring poison

sweet artesian water heals souls
wipes mud from blinded eyes
allows minds to see truth clearly
shatter opaque mirrors of evil
gaze into mirrors of eternity instead
discover divine truth by gazing within
find actualization as God's divine creation
align perspectives with God's
your eyes will mirror his truth upon your soul
drive the dark shadows of societal opinions away
reveal your inner light as a beacon to your soul
be a beacon for others that they too might know
in God's green garden when nurtured we grow
fill this eternal Eden with purified souls

Vacant Eyes

from the concrete porch I gaze at the Temple of the Winged Lion
I am greeted by the smiling sun at dawn beyond mauve cliffs
it rises over distant tombs, whose eyes follow their own shadows
what secrets will Bedouin trowels excavate this day
what surprises will we uncover as seen through Allat's vacant eyes

I step out out on the porch to gaze upon the Temple of the Winged Lion
secrets of the temple excavated through smiling eyes of Allat
from the concrete porch I gaze at the Temple of the Winged Lion

Darkness

You choose to love darkness
is that because it is what exists within?
I love you, darkness was part of your package
is that because of what exists within me?
darkness shadows our every step
outside the shadows there is warmth and light
why do you choose to walk in the shadows?
we fear the light when actions are unworthy
of the axioms of truth which dwell deep within
the foundation upon which we build our temples
we fear the light when we don't want others to see
it is easy to want to hide from prying, judgmental eyes
I do not judge you
I just want to understand why
within the darkness it is hard to see

Cost of Entropy

knees creak
hamstring burns
back spasms
thirteen pills
swallowed
by noon
entropy
is unkind
what wisdom
In my
suffering
do I find?
to find joy
In suffering
Is the paradox
of the divine

Eternal Eden

connections
eternal, through love
Christ's atonement heals connections
power of love heals the inner vessel
cleanses the inner vessel
fills the inner vessel
with the pure love of Christ
the true Christ dwells within

within the inner vessel
is a wellspring of healing love
pure love is the great creative force
pure love is the great healing force
there is a fountain within the soul
caked over by years of neglect
when primed will fill the inner vessel
with the healing power of love

love can heal connections
fallen into disrepair
by years of neglect
to neglect the inner vessel
is to starve the spirit
to starve the spirit is self-destructive
look within for healing
look within for eternal truth
look within for love to spring forth
to water life's garden
to grow Eternal Eden in your heart

Break

break chains which our souls bind
my weak, impetuous mind
strengthen my weakened walls
resistance when darkness falls
my inner vessel cleanse
upon perfect love depends
fill my vessel with truth and light
beacons to break me from blight
infestation of bodies delight
I must resist with all my might
Pain am I forced alone to bear?
generations stop, and at me stare
broken vessel so in need of repair
do not approach, you must beware
a quagmire so easily trapped in
vile, despicable, loathsome sin
turn instead to healing touch
break chains to free me from its clutch
resistance brings sweat upon my brow
the darkness of evil, turn away now
only one with divine power to heal
turn to the fire to refine my steel
resistance hardened by test of time
out of dark abyss I begin to climb
throw a stone, mirrors must break
only one way in darkness to forsake
break chains that remain to restrain
with perfect love no longer refrain

Break Spiritual Chains

noxious poison to bind the soul
drag it down to the gulf of misery and endless woe
opinion's forge chains of doom
forged of twisted perspectives of reality
deformed images of inner being
like gazing into a distorted mirror of the soul
pernicious thoughts forge chains
obscure divine perspectives
filled with enough deadly poison
to obscure inner light needed to guide
as spiritually poisonous as the beautiful oleander flower
is deadly
so lovely, yet how destructive to self
poison is found in pernicious thoughts
poison is found in evil doubts and fears
who is to determine what is evil
society opposes spiritual truth
claims its non-existence
claims evil is a function of situational reality
society creates the shame, the doubts, the fears that
plague mankind
spiritual doubt is a plague on earth
as we forget self, deny inner truth
it is as dark a plague as black death
because it is Black Death
we are left to wander in strange paths
to be lost in mists of darkness
to be drowned in dark waters
of a raging river full of poison and death
thoughts, doubts, fears, shame
forge chains of death and hell
or cast deleterious thoughts aside
as if they are unwanted starfish along life's seashore

debris washes up on our seashores
cast it into the eternal flame
to rise to the heavens and touch the stars
if evil thoughts bring poisonous chains
virtue and perfect love must break those chains
virtue is spiritual power to cleanse souls, heal hearts
purity within breaks pernicious chains as it radiates outward
pure and perfect love is a healing balm of compassion
show compassion to heal another
you will heal yourself as well
empathetic actions lead to healing of self
to see into another's soul, to know their suffering
to share their pain, experience who they are
shine your inner light of love upon their souls
this is Christ like love called charity, pure and perfect love
only given to those who are meek and lowly of heart
true followers of the Savior of mankind, Jesus Christ
love as Christ loves, see as Christ sees, know as Christ knows
we break chains of death and hell as we seek to accomplish divine tasks
we have no power in and of ourselves except as from he who rules all
the God of love, the healing balm of Gilead
the source of living waters to heal
we are engraven upon the palms of his hands
living waters mixed with his atoning blood
faith in this life altering process sets one on the covenant path
promises made to mourn with those who mourn
my beloved wife died, so I mourn
my children mourn, when I comfort those in need of comfort

healing waters flow both ways, I to find comfort
show love to find healing, nurture tender souls to find peace

Chains of Death and Hell

chains of death and hell will drag you down into the gulf of misery and woe
spiritual poison binds the soul, obscures vision, darkness ensues
inner light obscured, we flounder, we die spiritually
a slow agonizing death, we are lost to ourselves
break chains by seeking inner truth
break chains by shedding shame foisted upon us by society
break chains by igniting the flame of inner truth
truth's source is divinity, we are divine
doubts and fears drown our divinity in muddied waters
we cannot know, we cannot see, we die, and cannot be
reach out with your mind and your heart to touch another
embrace healing by sharing self with another
not to gratify lustful ambitions and desires
solely seek the healing welfare of another
to break chains of death and hell you must shed selfishness
embrace selflessness instead, embrace virtue of pure and perfect love
throw yourself into the flames of purity to temper your heart with love
selfish, self-centered, self-serving actions are consumed in the flames
find true compassionate love instead, love that binds souls, love that heals
nurture virtuous thoughts, cast aside unwanted starfish that litter your life
embrace divine truth, which can only be found by delving deep within self
look past doubts and fears, cast aside shame and guilt that obscure vision

delve deeper, then delve some more, see your inner truth
find your inner Christ, uncover your inner Buddha,
discover your divine truth
all chains will disintegrate, fall to the side as if turned to ashes and dust
let them blind your mind and encumber your soul no longer
look, see, know, understand, this is truth, this is life eternal
chains shattered, divine perspective revealed
healing love embraced, inner truth actualized, freedom of soul achieved

Bedouin's Love Song

I arise before the sun
so I might feel your kiss at dawn
your sun rises through the morning
I wander your ridges and dykes
seek out shrubs and grasses
you provide as sustenance to my herds
your cool cisterns quench my thirst
from underground reservoirs of your divine blood
it is your waters that make my existence possible
I live on the edge of existence
where my slightest misstep
could land me in an early grave
carved into the face of your dry, dusty floor
I am careful, ever wary
for I know your beauty is born of your savagery
you require all I have to give
I will never disrespect you
for I know the cost, instead I am ever grateful
for I know you are demanding, yet forgiving
when your heat scorches the dry earth
I find refuge in my goat hair tent
here my tea brews and my mansaf is prepared
never frightened of you, I embrace all challenges you present
I will not tempt fate, I will never challenge your dominion
I am at your mercy, but I am here with you
for I am familiar with your ways, with what makes you desirable
when the sun sets, I stand and gaze at your lovely silhouette
your red, orange sunset etches itself upon my mind
I need no canvas, my memory of you at sunset is enough

such truths never fade from my soul
I sing my love song to you
yet no notes emerge from my throat
this song is sung only in my heart
even as the Arabian wolf howls
and the Fennec Fox cries
throughout the moonlight night
when your rains fall in a deluge
flash foods fill your wadis and siqs
and a new kind of death stalks my Bedouin home
I will sing praises to your name for the tufts of green
which grow amidst your red, yellow, and mauve
sandstone outcrops
to provide fresh grazing for my goats and sheep
you are dangerous, you are beautiful, you are deadly
you are my mistress, desert is your name
I sing praises of love to hallow you, my love, my life, my
home

Be...

be as careful as a scurrying rabbit seeking a burrow as a hawk circles
be as alert as an impala watching a cheetah approach
be as courteous as orange emperor tulips bending before the wind and rain
be as patient as a caterpillar spinning a cocoon
be as fluid as a condor soaring amidst the snow packed peaks
be as shapeable as a deep arroyo cut by mountain storms
be as receptive as a mother's womb to a lover's seed
be as clear as a still pond awaiting winter's frost
be as grateful as the desert receiving anticipated rain
be as submissive as a dangling leaf awaiting a gust of wind

Do you grasp inner truth like fish gills gasp for water
when a brook trout is returned to a stream?
Do you have patience enough to watch the grass grow?
Can you remain unmoving at a timid deer's approach?
Can you anticipate self-actualization the way a robin
anticipates its song in spring?

look within to find your source of truth, buried deep
like an underground lake hidden within a lonely cave
acknowledge your source of divine truth
as if gazing into the night sky to reveal cosmic answers
discover you aren't as alone as you think you are
humanity is defined not by actions alone
but by our very thoughts and dreams
humanity is defined by inner reality
reflected through outward intentions to act
be true to self, be guided by spiritual truth

doubt not, fear not, look past opaque mirrors
gaze into the mirrors of eternity instead
to see all the beautiful possibilities that you can ever be

At-Oneness

oneness
spiritual manifestations
trembling souls of mankind
as if divine earthquakes
shake sacred ground of spirituality
opposing plates collide
fuse and unify
disparate parts united
to make discrete parts whole
joined like pieces of a cosmic puzzle
like strands of existence
in a web of life
in a sociality of at-oneness
forced to fit, forged to match
bound by virtue and perfect love
knit at-oneness with divine blood
sacrifice of pure white lamb without blemish
brings all things together at-oneness
sacrifice of broken hearts
sacrifice of contrite spirits

pave the way to at-oneness
crown of thorns placed
innocent blood shed
makes unity of souls possible
resurrection, rebirth
through at-oneness with the divine
burdens borne, prices paid
eternal possibilities realized
forged in the light of truth and right
pure and perfect love proclaimed
an anthem from angelic voices, heaven sent
faith ensures at-oneness is complete
hope burns bright in hearts and minds
divine love sheds itself
in hearts' of children of men
to bind many at-one in Zion
sociality of pure in heart to dwell in Zion
one in truth, one in love, one in light, at-oneness

Anasazi Connections

ancients connected in a web
checkered fields of cultivated maize
each colored thread in
complex geometric weaves connects
as each line of decoration
covering slip ware pottery

stories trickle down through time
myths to connect ancient to modern
to remember who they were
who they are, who we are
connected by culture and myth
as connected by genetic code

painted faces, feathers, and war drums
echoing from ancient pueblos
through hogans and kivas
into teepees with buffalo skin blankets
strewn upon the ground
for comfort and warmth
chants and sun dances connected
people so abundant, now sparse

I have no war drum connections
I only sing in the congregation
my connections rolled across the prairie
pitiful wagons, cold and miserable
barely a tattered blanket to give warmth
sickness and disease rampant
scarcely meal enough for a biscuit
frozen corpses discovered at dawn
infant dead buried beneath prairie sod
yet these pioneer connections persevered

make possible my mere existence

my connections follow a path of persecution
a proud people who would rather carve
out a feeble existence in a desert wilderness
Anasazi disappeared in this painted land
a people thrived, then nothing
Ute, Navajo, Hopi, Paiute, Goshute
Struggled for survival before
my ancestral connections
invaded their lands

two very different people connected
by persecution and deprivation
forced out, forced west
displace another, connected

predatory man takes what he wants
little conscience to question
relegate others to extinction, nonexistence
at times I feel relegated to nonexistence
existence that matters not
if one other person cares
can it really be nonexistence
only if all connections are severed
can we truly disappear

Anasazi connections existed
tied to nature as one people
to disappear without a trace
when were their connections severed?
if we sever our connections
to things which matter most,
what will be our eternal fate?
connections help define us

connections make us whole
connections keep us human
the sands of the desert connect me
to Anasazi ancients who dwelt here before
people erased by time
if we choose to erase another
what does that make us?
we may as well erase ourselves
in a very real sense we do

Agony of Mind

in agony of mind and soul
for peace and comfort where do you go
trials and troubles wrack your mind
poisonous doubts your pains define
burden so dark, loathsome, and complete
tears you up inside with torment replete
with all the fears waiting in dark mists
darkness fills mind, try to resist
I reach to you to touch your heart
Why did you leave me? why did we part?
I too feel loss and agony of pain
descends upon my soul like acid rain
my love for you exists in me still
thoughts of you break my will
I consider the love you and I share
passion so intense, our hearts bare
my mind reaches out to feel your torment
in deepest compassion I imbibe your scent
I tell you what is here within
not think it wrong, nor consider it sin
healing love is what I nurture for you inside
so from outstretched arms please don't hide
let me share the agony of your mind
bring peace to your soul, hearts aligned
let my compassion burn with blue, white heat
to ignite your heart with passion sweet
heal the agony which torments you
dry your tears like sunlight on dew
drive darkness out with hope's bright flame
declare open love with no shame
I beg you listen, I am here
realize in your heart I am so near
just look within and find this truth

mirrored in your heart is my life's proof
love we shared we can know again
I bear this truth with my heart's pen
I ask you my sweet let me drive agony away
let's embrace our future as a bright, new day

Evolutionary Transition

Cytoplasm ignites through prokaryotic transition
snowballing through eons of time to spring forth
through cognitive translation onto the printed page
bearing forth truths of evolutionary progression

Cells divide through meiosis, evolve into specialization
as function dictates form, Darwinian survival governs all
transition from simple into complex as speciation
branches
environment governs developmental selection to improve

Branches of the evolutionary tree lead into multiple
deviations
leafy ferns descend from primitive forms branching forth
into needles and pines, leafs and flowers, evolutionary
transitions
successes and failures along the way as future takes shape

Short Verses and Haiku

Short Verses and Haiku

hardened diamonds encase molten lava, locked within
blocks natural flow of inner truth to consume falsehoods
like a starved lioness feasting on a downed wildebeest
vile assumptions obscure the light of divine reality
revelation's light cannot pierce such a hardened shell

***

look inside my head
Nothingness! Am I dead?
gaze into my heart instead

***

discovering inner truth
Is like excavating Petra's Temple of the Winged Lion
you never know what your trowel will uncover
when it first strikes earth

***

little lark in tree
do you warble soft for me
honeyed song of life

***

white winter's snow
evergreen bush clings so
sparrows sing on

***

distant bells ringing
sweet meadowlarks warbling
lovers come at dawn

***

snow blanket cedars
silently creeps frozen dawn
inspires gentle souls

***

sweet strawberry fields
beneath your naked flesh
bring me ecstasy

***

storm tossed on open sea
safe harbor I find in you
we climax at dawn

***

grey clouds overhead
lightning strikes hardened earth
rain on naked flesh

***

motorbike races
through hot empty desert
destiny embraced

***

vastness spreads below
emptiness of space and time
between colored sands

***

snow falls silently
shroud of white cathedrals
vaulted overhead

***

snow falls on pine trees
beckons laughter of children
sledding on hills

***

red roses on table
sweet smell of life beginning
joy consumes my soul

***

sweet smiling faces
pressed against the window pane
waiting for papa

***

woman is beauty
gracefully she moves through life
plucks love's sweet blossoms

***

stones' transparent ethereal emanation
float in the nexus of Eden's creation
fused by passion's gravitational immensity
fed by lovers' erotic desires pure intensity

***

evil festers in the hearts of the children of men
like poison, which gathers in a stone vessel
shatter the vessel and let the poison flow free

***

trials of time tempers steel
razor sharp edge to slice clean
a two edged sword of truth

***

kneel on hallowed Rock
burning bush speaks
God's word revealed

***

heart shattered like a smashed vase
vessel of truth scattered at my feet
light to unite the pieces, make me whole
descends from celestial realm, cloaked in white
through the blood of the sacrificial lamb

***

to engraven stone choose the perfect chisel and the right mallet
creating a work of art by knapping chip by chip, chunk by chunk
to refine a character on life's stage needs a special kind of chisel and mallet
vicissitudes of life play the chisel, God wields the mallet to direct
God knows who we are, what bits of stone belong, what to knock off
What does God create when he engraves his image in your countenance?
surely something that the turmoil of time cannot not easily erase

***

I never saw an Arabian Oryx cross the desert floor
I've never watched unicorn prances in my backyard.

***

winged poetry among the clouds
floats gracefully around snow capped peaks
fluffy ballerinas in black feathered leotards
sunbeams as steps to pirouette into space
black swans would be so jealous of their majesty

red-breasted robin sings
yellow-breasted meadowlark warbles
snow melt flows
cherry trees awash in pink
spring awakens at dawn

***

branches drip
blue jay pecks melting snow
between green sprouts of wheat

***

opaque images
twisted and gnarled
like looking through
a fun house mirror
at selves and others

wounded desert
gaze beyond silhouetted horizons
with vacant, haunted eyes
through Orion's taut bow and beyond

vacant eyes
bronze Zeus in situ ponders
Petra's hidden secrets

***

withered lily
tortured hearts cast aside
crumpled at love's door

empty cave
warble lost on soundless wind
announces Easter's dawn

trickle of water
clumps of earth bar progress
of roots' descent

swans glide lazily
upon mirrored pond
bass nip skeeters beneath
dart between rocks and reeds
pursue minnows and perch
to fill their hungry need
so many truths hidden
from our corporeal eyes
so is the mirror on your soul
what secrets lurk below

***

temple spire glows
rays glisten off gilded doors
beckon wayfaring man of grief

***

heart of flame
my body touched by yours
brings deep arousal

***

eternal flame
aged eyes watch with glee
as children play

***

shattered mind
wander in mists of darkness
lost to true self

***

stooped back
heavy laden in pouring rain
counting tears on pebbles

***

golden angel
trumpet forth ancient truth
wind blown dust speaks

***

I no longer can forsake
power to set my soul to flight
to carry on life's fight
my soul's power to take flight

***

if I am nothing
how do you explain my existence
in space-time

***

virtue and truth
fruit of the divine
love gives us proof

***

opaque mirrors
rippled surface of a pond
hides decay beyond

***

slippery salmon
grizzly bear juggles future
with uncertain claws

***

winged condor
poetry floats among clouds
spies death below

***

distant bells ring
sweet meadowlarks sing
ecstasy at dawn

***

snow falls on cedars
silent before dawn
inspires my soul
could nothing question its own existence
yet earth spins on
regardless of what I do
my m just hasn't been transformed into e yet
in a flash of brilliant light
when it does

I'll still be something
Whether you see it any longer or not

***

with joyous wonder
I gaze into your
bright brown eyes and ponder
who you really are
with a sweet smile
as broad as the starry sky
on which you gaze
with childish delight

End of Short Poems

ABOUT THE AUTHOR

Thomas Fullmer is the author of several books, including his book of poetry, From the Fabric of My Mind, and his children's book, Roslyn, the Reluctant Rattlesnake. This is his second book of poetry. In his first book of poetry he spoke of his love for his wife, and the loss he felt after her passing away in September 2019. This book of poetry continues on that vein in celebrating her life and the love they shared.

www.ingramcontent.com/pod-product-compliance
Lightning Source LLC
LaVergne TN
LVHW091317150826
845673LV00006B/1683

* 9 7 9 8 6 4 8 0 7 8 2 5 3 *